CROCK·POT®
◆ THE ORIGINAL SLOW COOKER ◆

Family
FAVORITES

pil

Publications International, Ltd.

Pictured on the front cover: Slow Cooker Pizza Casserole *(page 152)*.

Pictured on the back cover *(left to right):* Chorizo Chili *(page 58)* and Easy Parmesan Chicken *(page 88)*.

ISBN: 978-1-4508-8899-8

Library of Congress Control Number: 2014936679

Manufactured in China.

8 7 6 5 4 3 2 1

Publications International, Ltd.

Contents

Slow Cooking 101

Slow Cooker Sizes

Smaller **CROCK-POT**® slow cookers—such as 1- to 3½-quart models—are the perfect size for cooking for singles, a couple, or empty-nesters (and also for serving dips).

While medium-size **CROCK-POT**® slow cookers (those holding somewhere between 3 quarts and 5 quarts) will easily cook enough food at a time to feed a small family, they're also convenient for holiday side dishes or appetizers.

Large **CROCK-POT**® slow cookers are great for large family dinners, holiday entertaining, and potluck suppers. A 6- to 7-quart model is ideal if you like to make meals in advance, or have dinner tonight and store leftovers for another day.

Types of Slow Cookers

Current **CROCK-POT**® slow cookers come equipped with many different features and benefits, from auto cook programs to stovetop-safe stoneware to timed programming. Visit **www.crockpot.com** to find the **CROCK-POT**® slow cooker that best suits your needs.

How you plan to use a **CROCK-POT**® slow cooker may affect the model you choose to purchase. For everyday cooking, choose a size large enough to serve your family. If you plan to use the **CROCK-POT**® slow cooker primarily for entertaining, choose one of the larger sizes. Basic **CROCK-POT**® slow cookers can hold as little as 16 ounces or as much as 7 quarts. The smallest sizes are great for keeping dips warm on a buffet, while the larger sizes can more readily fit large quantities of food and larger roasts.

Cooking, Stirring, and Food Safety

CROCK-POT® slow cookers are safe to leave unattended. The outer heating base may get hot as it cooks, but it should not pose a fire hazard. The heating element in the heating base functions at a low wattage and is safe for your countertops.

Your **CROCK-POT**® slow cooker should be filled about one-half to three-fourths full for most recipes unless otherwise instructed. Lean meats such as chicken or pork tenderloin will cook faster than meats with more connective tissue and fat such as beef chuck or pork shoulder. Bone-in meats will take longer than boneless cuts. Typical **CROCK-POT**® slow cooker dishes take approximately 7 to 8 hours to reach the simmer point on LOW and about 3 to 4 hours on HIGH. Once the vegetables and meat start to simmer and braise, their flavors will fully blend and meat will become fall-off-the-bone tender.

According to the USDA, all bacteria are killed at a temperature of 165°F. It's important to follow the recommended cooking times and not to open the lid often, especially early in the cooking process when heat is building up inside the unit. If you need to open the lid to check on your food or are adding additional ingredients, remember to allow additional cooking time if necessary to ensure food is cooked through and tender.

Large **CROCK-POT**® slow cookers, the 6- to 7-quart sizes, may benefit with a quick stir halfway through cook time to help distribute heat and promote even cooking. It's usually unnecessary to stir at all, as even ½ cup liquid will help to distribute heat and the stoneware is the perfect medium for holding food at an even temperature throughout the cooking process.

Oven-Safe

All **CROCK-POT**® slow cooker removable stoneware inserts may (without their lids) be used safely in ovens at up to 400°F. Also, all **CROCK-POT**® slow cookers are microwavable without their lids. If you own another brand

slow cooker, please refer to your owner's manual for specific stoneware cooking medium tolerances.

Frozen Food

Frozen food or partially frozen food can be successfully cooked in a **CROCK-POT**® slow cooker; however, it will require longer cooking time than the same recipe made with fresh food. It's almost always preferable to thaw frozen food prior to placing it in the **CROCK-POT**® slow cooker. Using an instant-read thermometer is recommended to ensure meat is fully cooked through.

Pasta and Rice

If you're converting a recipe that calls for uncooked pasta, cook the pasta on the stovetop just until slightly tender before adding to the **CROCK-POT**® slow cooker. If you are converting a recipe that calls for cooked rice, stir in raw rice with other ingredients; add ¼ cup extra liquid per ¼ cup of raw rice.

Beans

Beans must be softened completely before combining with sugar and/or acidic foods. Sugar and acid have a hardening effect on beans and will prevent softening. Fully cooked canned beans may be used as a substitute for dried beans.

Vegetables

Root vegetables often cook more slowly than meat. Cut vegetables accordingly to cook at the same rate as meat—large or small, or lean versus marbled—and place near the sides or bottom of the stoneware to facilitate cooking.

Herbs

Fresh herbs add flavor and color when added at the end of the cooking cycle; if added at the beginning, many fresh herbs' flavor will dissipate over long cook times. Ground and/or dried herbs and spices work well in slow cooking and may be added at the beginning, and for dishes with shorter cook times, hearty fresh herbs such as rosemary and thyme hold up well. The flavor power of all herbs and spices can vary greatly depending on their particular strength and shelf life. Use chili powders and garlic powder sparingly, as these can sometimes intensify over the long cook times. Always taste the finished dish and correct seasonings including salt and pepper.

Liquids

It is not necessary to use more than ½ to 1 cup liquid in most instances since juices in meats and vegetables are retained more in slow cooking than in conventional cooking. Excess liquid can be cooked down and concentrated after slow cooking on the stovetop or by removing meat and vegetables from stoneware, stirring in one of the following thickeners, and setting the slow cooker to HIGH. Cook on HIGH for approximately 15 minutes or until juices are thickened.

Flour: All-purpose flour is often used to thicken soups or stews. Stir cold water into the flour in a small bowl until smooth. With the **CROCK-POT**® slow cooker on HIGH, whisk the flour mixture into the liquid in the **CROCK-POT**® slow cooker. Cover; cook on HIGH 15 minutes or until the mixture is thickened.

Cornstarch: Cornstarch gives sauces a clear, shiny appearance; it's used most often for sweet dessert sauces and stir-fry sauces.

Stir cold water into the cornstarch in a small bowl until the cornstarch dissolves. Quickly stir this mixture into the liquid in the **CROCK-POT**® slow cooker; the sauce will thicken as soon as the liquid boils. Cornstarch breaks down with too much heat, so never add it at the beginning of the slow cooking process, and turn off the heat as soon as the sauce thickens.

Arrowroot: Arrowroot (or arrowroot flour) comes from the root of a tropical plant that is dried and ground to a powder; it produces a thick clear sauce. Those who are allergic to wheat often use it in place of flour. Place arrowroot in a small bowl or cup and stir in cold water until the mixture is smooth. Quickly stir this mixture into the liquid in the **CROCK-POT**® slow cooker. Arrowroot thickens below the boiling point, so it even works well in a **CROCK-POT**® slow cooker on LOW. Too much stirring can break down an arrowroot mixture.

Tapioca: Tapioca is a starchy substance extracted from the root of the cassava plant. Its greatest advantage is that it withstands long cooking, making it an ideal choice for slow cooking. Add it at the beginning of cooking and you'll get a clear thickened sauce in the finished dish. Dishes using tapioca as a thickener are best cooked on the LOW setting; tapioca may become stringy when boiled for a long time.

Milk

Milk, cream and sour cream break down during extended cooking. When possible, add them during the last 15 to 30 minutes of cooking, until just heated through. Condensed soups may be substituted for milk and can cook for extended times.

Fish

Fish is delicate and should be stirred in gently during the last 15 to 30 minutes of cooking time. Cover and cook just until cooked through and serve immediately.

Baked Goods

If you wish to prepare bread, cakes, or pudding cakes in a **CROCK-POT**® slow cooker, you may want to purchase a covered, vented metal cake pan accessory for your **CROCK-POT**® slow cooker. You can also use any straight-sided soufflé dish or deep cake pan that will fit into the stoneware of your unit. Baked goods can be prepared directly in the stoneware; however, they can be a little difficult to remove from the insert, so follow the recipe directions carefully.

CROCK·POT®

◆ THE ORIGINAL SLOW COOKER ◆

Pizza Fondue (page 32)

Hoisin Barbecue Chicken Sliders (page 22)

Finger Foods

Honey-Glazed Chicken Wings (page 26)

Barbecued Meatballs

2 pounds ground beef

1⅓ cups ketchup, divided

3 tablespoons seasoned dry bread crumbs

1 egg, lightly beaten

2 tablespoons dried minced onion

¾ teaspoon garlic salt

½ teaspoon black pepper

1 cup packed brown sugar

1 can (6 ounces) tomato paste

¼ cup soy sauce

¼ cup cider vinegar

1½ teaspoons hot pepper sauce

Sliced green bell peppers (optional)

1. Preheat oven to 350°F. Combine beef, ⅓ cup ketchup, bread crumbs, egg, dried onion, garlic salt and black pepper in medium bowl. Mix lightly but thoroughly; shape into 1-inch meatballs.

2. Place meatballs in two 15×10-inch jelly-roll pans or shallow roasting pans. Bake 18 minutes or until browned. Remove to **CROCK-POT®** slow cooker using slotted spoon.

3. Mix remaining 1 cup ketchup, brown sugar, tomato paste, soy sauce, vinegar and hot pepper sauce in medium bowl. Pour over meatballs. Cover; cook on LOW 4 hours. Stir in bell peppers during last 20 minutes of cooking, if desired.

Makes about 4 dozen meatballs

Barbecued Franks: Arrange two 12-ounce packages or three 8-ounce packages of cocktail franks in **CROCK-POT®** slow cooker. Combine 1 cup ketchup, brown sugar, tomato paste, soy sauce, vinegar and hot pepper sauce in medium bowl; pour over franks. Cover; cook on LOW 4 hours. Stir in bell peppers during last 20 minutes of cooking, if desired. Makes 12 to 14 servings.

Angelic Deviled Eggs

6 eggs

¼ cup cottage cheese

3 tablespoons ranch dressing

2 teaspoons Dijon mustard

2 tablespoons minced fresh chives or dill

1 tablespoon diced well-drained pimientos or roasted red pepper

1. Place eggs in single layer in bottom of **CROCK-POT®** slow cooker; add just enough water to cover tops of eggs. Cover; cook on LOW 3½ hours. Rinse and drain eggs under cold water; peel when cool enough to handle.

2. Cut eggs in half lengthwise. Remove yolks, reserving 3 yolk halves. Discard remaining yolks or reserve for another use. Place egg whites, cut sides up, on serving plate; cover with plastic wrap. Refrigerate while preparing filling.

3. Combine cottage cheese, dressing, mustard and reserved yolk halves in food processor or blender; process until smooth. (Or, place in small bowl and mash with fork until well blended.) Remove cheese mixture to small bowl; stir in chives and pimientos. Spoon into egg whites. Cover and refrigerate at least 1 hour before serving.

Makes 12 servings

Cereal Snack Mix

6 tablespoons unsalted butter, melted

2 tablespoons curry powder

2 tablespoons soy sauce

1 tablespoon sugar

1 tablespoon paprika

2 teaspoons ground cumin

½ teaspoon salt

5 cups rice squares cereal

5 cups corn squares cereal

1 cup tiny pretzels

⅓ cup peanuts

1. Pour butter in **CROCK-POT**® slow cooker. Stir in curry powder, soy sauce, sugar, paprika, cumin and salt. Stir in cereal, pretzels and peanuts. Cook, uncovered, on HIGH 45 minutes, stirring often.

2. Turn **CROCK-POT**® slow cooker to LOW. Cook, uncovered, on LOW 3 to 4 hours, stirring often. Turn off heat. Let cool completely.

Makes 20 servings

tip

Stirring the Cereal Snack Mix often during cooking prevents it from scorching.

Nacho Dip

1 tablespoon vegetable oil

1 onion, chopped

2 pounds ground beef

2 cans (about 15 ounces *each*) black beans, rinsed and drained

1 can (28 ounces) diced tomatoes

1 can (about 15 ounces) refried beans

1 can (about 15 ounces) cream-style corn

3 cloves garlic, minced

1 package (1 ounce) taco seasoning

  Tortilla chips

  Queso blanco

1. Heat oil in large skillet over medium-high heat. Add onion; cook 2 to 3 minutes or until translucent. Add beef; brown 6 to 8 minutes, stirring to break up meat. Drain fat.

2. Stir beef mixture, black beans, tomatoes, refried beans, corn, garlic and taco seasoning into **CROCK-POT**® slow cooker. Cover; cook on LOW 5 to 6 hours or on HIGH 2½ to 3 hours. Serve on tortilla chips. Sprinkle with queso blanco.

Makes 10 cups

Chipotle Turkey Sloppy Joe Sliders

1 pound turkey Italian
    sausage, casings
    removed

1 package (14 ounces) frozen
    green and red bell pepper
    strips with onions,
    thawed

1 can (6 ounces) tomato paste

1 tablespoon quick-cooking
    tapioca

1 tablespoon minced canned
    chipotle peppers in
    adobo sauce, plus
    1 tablespoon sauce

2 teaspoons ground cumin

½ teaspoon dried thyme

12 corn muffins or small dinner
    rolls, split and toasted

1. Brown sausage in large skillet over medium-high heat 6 to 8 minutes, stirring to break up meat. Remove to **CROCK-POT®** slow cooker using slotted spoon.

2. Stir in pepper strips with onions, tomato paste, tapioca, chipotle peppers with sauce, cumin and thyme. Cover; cook on LOW 8 to 10 hours. Serve on corn muffins.

Makes 12 sliders

Easiest Three-Cheese Fondue

2 cups (8 ounces) shredded Cheddar cheese

¾ cup milk

½ cup crumbled blue cheese

1 package (3 ounces) cream cheese, cut into cubes

¼ cup finely chopped onion

1 tablespoon all-purpose flour

1 tablespoon butter

2 cloves garlic, minced

4 to 6 drops hot pepper sauce

⅛ teaspoon ground red pepper

Breadsticks and assorted cut-up fresh vegetables

1. Combine Cheddar cheese, milk, blue cheese, cream cheese, onion, flour, butter, garlic, hot pepper sauce and ground red pepper in **CROCK-POT**® slow cooker. Cover; cook on LOW 2 to 2½ hours, stirring halfway through cooking time.

2. Turn **CROCK-POT**® slow cooker to HIGH. Cover; cook on HIGH 1 to 1½ hours or until heated through. Serve with breadsticks and vegetables.

Makes 8 servings

Salsa-Style Wings

2 tablespoons oil
1½ pounds chicken wings (about 18 wings)
2 cups salsa
¼ cup packed brown sugar

1. Heat oil in large skillet over medium-high heat. Add wings in batches; cook 3 to 4 minutes or until wings are brown on all sides. Remove to **CROCK-POT®** slow cooker. Combine salsa and brown sugar in medium bowl; stir until well blended. Pour over wings.

2. Cover; cook on LOW 5 to 6 hours or on HIGH 2 to 3 hours. Serve with salsa mixture.

Makes 18 wings

Hoisin Barbecue Chicken Sliders

(pictured on page 8)

⅔ cup hoisin sauce
⅓ cup barbecue sauce
3 tablespoons quick-cooking tapioca
1 tablespoon sugar
1 tablespoon soy sauce
¼ teaspoon red pepper flakes
12 boneless, skinless chicken thighs (3 to 3½ pounds total)
16 dinner rolls or Hawaiian sweet rolls, split
½ medium red onion, finely chopped (optional)
Sliced pickles (optional)

1. Combine hoisin sauce, barbecue sauce, tapioca, sugar, soy sauce and red pepper flakes in **CROCK-POT®** slow cooker; mix well. Add chicken. Cover; cook on LOW 8 to 9 hours.

2. Remove chicken to cutting board; shred with two forks. Return shredded chicken (and any sauce that accumulates on cutting board) to **CROCK-POT®** slow cooker; stir well. Spoon ¼ cup chicken and sauce onto each roll. Top each with chopped onion and pickles, if desired.

Makes 16 sliders

Salsa-Style Wings

Mini Carnitas Tacos

1½ pounds boneless pork loin,
cut into 1-inch cubes

1 onion, finely chopped

½ cup chicken broth

1 tablespoon chili powder

2 teaspoons ground cumin

1 teaspoon dried oregano

½ teaspoon minced canned
chipotle peppers in
adobo sauce

½ cup pico de gallo

2 tablespoons chopped fresh
cilantro

½ teaspoon salt

12 (6-inch) corn or flour tortillas

¾ cup (3 ounces) shredded
sharp Cheddar cheese

3 tablespoons sour cream

1. Combine pork, onion, broth, chili powder, cumin, oregano and chipotle peppers in **CROCK-POT**® slow cooker. Cover; cook on LOW 6 hours or on HIGH 3 hours. Pour off excess cooking liquid.

2. Remove pork to cutting board; shred with two forks. Return to **CROCK-POT**® slow cooker. Stir in pico de gallo, cilantro and salt. Cover; keep warm on LOW or WARM setting.

3. Cut three circles from each tortilla with 2-inch biscuit cutter. Top each with pork, cheese and sour cream. Serve warm.

Makes 12 servings

tip

Carnitas, or "little meats" in Spanish, are a festive way to spice up any gathering. Carnitas traditionally include a large amount of lard, but slow cooking makes the dish healthier by eliminating the need to add lard, oil or fat, while keeping the meat tender and delicious.

Bacon-Wrapped Fingerling Potatoes

1 pound fingerling potatoes

2 tablespoons olive oil

1 tablespoon minced fresh thyme

½ teaspoon black pepper

¼ teaspoon paprika

½ pound bacon slices, cut crosswise into halves

¼ cup chicken broth

1. Toss potatoes with oil, thyme, pepper and paprika in large bowl. Wrap half slice of bacon tightly around each potato.

2. Heat large skillet over medium heat; add potatoes. Reduce heat to medium-low; cook until lightly browned and bacon has tightened around potatoes. Place potatoes in **CROCK-POT®** slow cooker. Add broth. Cover; cook on HIGH 3 hours.

Makes 4 to 6 servings

Honey-Glazed Chicken Wings

(pictured on page 9)

3 tablespoons vegetable oil, divided

3 pounds chicken wings

1 cup honey

½ cup soy sauce

1 clove garlic, minced

2 tablespoons tomato paste

2 teaspoons water

1 teaspoon sugar

1 teaspoon black pepper

1. Heat 1½ tablespoons oil in skillet over medium heat. Add wings in batches; cook 1 to 2 minutes on each side or until browned. Remove to **CROCK-POT®** slow cooker using slotted spoon.

2. Combine honey, soy sauce, remaining 1½ tablespoons oil and garlic in medium bowl. Whisk in tomato paste, water, sugar and pepper. Pour sauce over wings. Cover; cook on LOW 6 to 8 hours or on HIGH 3 to 4 hours.

Makes 6 to 8 servings

Bacon-Wrapped Fingerling Potatoes

Hot Broccoli Cheese Dip

½ cup (1 stick) butter

6 stalks celery, sliced

2 onions, chopped

2 cans (4 ounces *each*) sliced
   mushrooms, drained

¼ cup plus 2 tablespoons
   all-purpose flour

2 cans (10¾ ounces *each*)
   condensed cream of
   celery soup, undiluted

5 to 6 ounces garlic cheese,
   cut into cubes

2 packages (10 ounces *each*)
   frozen broccoli

French bread slices, bell
   pepper strips, cherry
   tomatoes

1. Melt butter in large skillet over medium heat. Add celery, onions and mushrooms; cook and stir 5 to 7 minutes or until onions are translucent. Stir in flour; cook 2 to 3 minutes. Remove to **CROCK-POT**® slow cooker.

2. Stir in soup, cheese and broccoli. Cover; cook on HIGH 45 minutes or until cheese is melted, stirring every 15 minutes.

3. Turn **CROCK-POT**® slow cooker to LOW. Cover; cook on LOW 2 to 4 hours. Serve warm with bread and vegetables.

Makes about 6 cups

Mini Meatball Grinders

1 can (about 14 ounces) diced
    tomatoes, drained and
    juices reserved

1 can (8 ounces) tomato sauce

¼ cup chopped onion

2 tablespoons tomato paste

1 teaspoon Italian seasoning

1 pound ground chicken

½ cup fresh whole wheat or
    white bread crumbs
    (1 slice bread)

1 egg white, lightly beaten

3 tablespoons finely chopped
    fresh Italian parsley

2 cloves garlic, minced

¼ teaspoon salt

⅛ teaspoon black pepper

    Nonstick cooking spray

4 hard rolls, split and toasted

3 tablespoons grated
    Parmesan cheese
    (optional)

1. Combine tomatoes, ½ cup reserved juice, tomato sauce, onion, tomato paste and Italian seasoning in **CROCK-POT®** slow cooker. Cover; cook on LOW 3 to 4 hours.

2. Prepare meatballs halfway through cooking time. Combine chicken, bread crumbs, egg white, parsley, garlic, salt and pepper in medium bowl; mix well. Shape mixture into 12 meatballs. Cover; refrigerate 30 minutes.

3. Spray medium skillet with cooking spray; heat over medium heat. Add meatballs; cook 8 to 10 minutes or until well browned on all sides. Remove meatballs to **CROCK-POT®** slow cooker using slotted spoon. Cover; cook on LOW 1 to 2 hours or until no longer pink in center.

4. Place 3 meatballs in each roll; top with sauce. Sprinkle with cheese, if desired. Cut each roll into thirds.

Makes 12 servings

Spicy Sweet and Sour Cocktail Franks

**2 packages (8 ounces *each*)
  cocktail franks**
½ cup ketchup or chili sauce
½ cup apricot preserves
1 teaspoon hot pepper sauce

Combine cocktail franks, ketchup, preserves and hot pepper sauce in 1½-quart **CROCK-POT®** slow cooker; mix well. Cover; cook on LOW 2 to 3 hours.

Makes 10 to 12 servings

Pizza Fondue

(pictured on page 8)

½ pound bulk Italian sausage
1 cup chopped onion
**2 jars (26 ounces *each*)
  meatless pasta sauce**
**4 ounces thinly sliced ham,
  finely chopped**
**1 package (3 ounces) sliced
  pepperoni, finely
  chopped**
¼ teaspoon red pepper flakes
**1 pound mozzarella cheese,
  cut into ¾-inch cubes**
**1 loaf Italian or French bread,
  cut into 1-inch cubes**

1. Brown sausage and onion in large skillet over medium-high heat 6 to 8 minutes, stirring to break up meat. Remove to **CROCK-POT®** slow cooker using slotted spoon.

2. Stir in pasta sauce, ham, pepperoni and red pepper flakes. Cover; cook on LOW 3 to 4 hours. Serve with cheese and bread cubes.

Makes 20 to 25 servings

Spicy Sweet and Sour Cocktail Franks

Parmesan Ranch Snack Mix

3 cups corn or rice cereal
squares

2 cups oyster crackers

1 package (5 ounces) bagel
chips, broken in half

1½ cups mini pretzel twists

1 cup pistachio nuts

2 tablespoons grated
Parmesan cheese

¼ cup (½ stick) butter, melted

1 package (1 ounce) dry ranch
salad dressing mix

½ teaspoon garlic powder

1. Combine cereal, crackers, bagel chips, pretzels, nuts and cheese in **CROCK-POT®** slow cooker; mix gently.

2. Combine butter, salad dressing mix and garlic powder in small bowl. Pour over cereal mixture; toss lightly to coat. Cover; cook on LOW 3 hours.

3. Stir gently. Cook, uncovered, on LOW 30 minutes.

Makes about 9½ cups

Honey Ribs

1 can (about 14 ounces)
    beef broth
½ cup water
3 tablespoons soy sauce
2 tablespoons honey
2 tablespoons maple syrup
2 tablespoons barbecue sauce
½ teaspoon dry mustard
2 pounds pork baby back ribs,
    trimmed and cut into
    3- to 4-rib portions

1. Combine broth, water, soy sauce, honey, syrup, barbecue sauce and mustard in **CROCK-POT®** slow cooker; stir to blend. Add ribs.

2. Cover; cook on LOW 6 to 8 hours or on HIGH 4 to 6 hours. Serve with sauce.

Makes 4 servings

Barbecue Sloppy Joe Dip

2 teaspoons olive oil
¾ pound ground beef
⅓ cup finely chopped onion
1 clove garlic, minced
¼ teaspoon dried oregano
¼ cup barbecue sauce
2 tablespoons ketchup
2 teaspoons packed brown
    sugar
2 teaspoons cider vinegar
¾ cup (3 ounces) shredded
    Monterey Jack cheese
1 tablespoon chopped fresh
    cilantro
    Sliced baguettes

1. Heat oil in large skillet over medium-high heat. Add beef; cook and stir 6 to 8 minutes or until browned. Stir in onion, garlic and oregano; cook 4 minutes. Remove from heat. Stir in barbecue sauce, ketchup, brown sugar and vinegar. Let cool 2 minutes; stir in cheese.

2. Remove to **CROCK-POT® LITTLE DIPPER®** slow cooker. Cover; heat 1 hour or until cheese is melted. Stir well; sprinkle with cilantro. Serve with baguettes.

Makes about 1½ cups

Honey Ribs

Easy Chili (page 56)

Potato Soup (page 68)

Soups and Chilies

Simmered Split Pea Soup (page 64)

Hearty Sausage and Tortellini Soup

3 hot Italian sausages, casings removed

3 sweet Italian sausages, casings removed

5 cups chicken broth

1 can (about 14 ounces) diced tomatoes with garlic and oregano

1 can (about 8 ounces) tomato sauce

1 large onion, chopped

2 medium carrots, chopped

1 teaspoon seasoned salt

½ teaspoon Italian seasoning

¼ teaspoon black pepper

1 package (9 ounces) refrigerated cheese tortellini

1 medium zucchini, chopped

2 cups broccoli, chopped

1. Cook sausages in large skillet over medium-high heat 8 to 10 minutes. Drain fat. Add sausages, broth, diced tomatoes, tomato sauce, onion, carrots, seasoned salt, Italian seasoning and pepper to **CROCK-POT®** slow cooker. Cover; cook on LOW 6 to 8 hours or on HIGH 3 to 4 hours.

2. Meanwhile, cook tortellini according to package directions. Add tortellini, zucchini and broccoli to **CROCK-POT®** slow cooker during last 15 to 20 minutes of cooking.

Makes 6 to 8 servings

Classic Chili

1½ pounds ground beef

1½ cups chopped onion

1 cup chopped green bell pepper

2 cloves garlic, minced

3 cans (about 15 ounces *each*) dark red kidney beans, rinsed and drained

2 cans (about 15 ounces *each*) tomato sauce

1 can (about 14 ounces) diced tomatoes

2 to 3 teaspoons chili powder

1 to 2 teaspoons ground mustard

¾ teaspoon dried basil

½ teaspoon black pepper

1 to 2 dried red chiles (optional)

1. Brown beef, onion, bell pepper and garlic in large skillet over medium-high heat, stirring to break up meat. Remove beef mixture to **CROCK-POT®** slow cooker using slotted spoon.

2. Add beans, tomato sauce, tomatoes, chili powder, mustard, basil, black pepper and chiles, if desired, to **CROCK-POT®** slow cooker; mix well. Cover; cook on LOW 8 to 10 hours or on HIGH 4 to 5 hours. If used, remove chiles before serving.

Makes 6 servings

Asian Sugar Snap Pea Soup

2 tablespoons peanut or
   canola oil

4 to 5 new potatoes, coarsely
   chopped

2 green onions, chopped

1 medium carrot, thinly sliced

1 stalk celery, thinly sliced

1 leek, thinly sliced

5 cups water

2 cups broccoli, washed and
   cut into florets

1 tablespoon lemon juice

1 tablespoon soy sauce

1 teaspoon ground coriander

1 teaspoon ground cumin

1 teaspoon prepared
   horseradish

⅛ teaspoon ground red pepper

1 cup fresh sugar snap peas,
   shelled, rinsed and
   drained

4 cups cooked brown rice

1. Heat oil in large skillet over medium heat. Add potatoes, green onions, carrot, celery and leek; cook and stir 10 to 12 minutes or until vegetables begin to soften.

2. Remove to **CROCK-POT®** slow cooker. Add water, broccoli, lemon juice, soy sauce, coriander, cumin, horseradish and ground red pepper. Cover; cook on LOW 5 to 6 hours or on HIGH 2 to 3 hours.

3. Stir in peas. Cover; cook on HIGH 15 minutes or until peas are crisp-tender. To serve, portion rice into four bowls. Ladle soup over rice and serve immediately.

Makes 4 servings

Weeknight Chili

1 pound ground beef or turkey

1 package (about 1 ounce) chili seasoning mix

1 can (about 15 ounces) red kidney beans, rinsed and drained

1 can (about 14 ounces) diced tomatoes with mild green chiles

1 can (8 ounces) tomato sauce

1 cup (4 ounces) shredded Cheddar cheese (optional)

Chopped green onion (optional)

1. Brown beef in large skillet over medium-high heat 6 to 8 minutes, stirring to break up meat. Drain fat. Stir in seasoning mix.

2. Place beef mixture, beans, tomatoes and tomato sauce in **CROCK-POT®** slow cooker. Cover; cook on LOW 4 to 6 hours or on HIGH 2 to 3 hours. Garnish with cheese and green onion.

Makes 4 servings

Mother's Sausage and Vegetable Soup

1 can (about 15 ounces)
   black beans, rinsed and
   drained
1 can (about 14 ounces) diced
   tomatoes
1 can (10¾ ounces) condensed
   cream of mushroom
   soup, undiluted
½ pound smoked turkey
   sausage, cut into ½-inch
   slices
2 cups diced potato
1 cup chopped onion
1 cup chopped red bell pepper
½ cup water
2 teaspoons prepared
   horseradish
2 teaspoons honey
1 teaspoon dried basil

Combine beans, tomatoes, soup, turkey sausage, potato, onion, pepper, water, horseradish, honey and basil in **CROCK-POT®** slow cooker; stir to blend. Cover; cook on LOW 7 to 8 hours.

Makes 6 to 8 servings

Chili with Turkey and Beans

2 cans (about 15 ounces *each*) red kidney beans, rinsed and drained

2 cans (about 14 ounces *each*) whole tomatoes, drained

1 pound cooked ground turkey

1 can (about 15 ounces) black beans, rinsed and drained

1 can (12 ounces) tomato sauce

1 cup finely chopped onion

1 cup finely chopped celery

1 cup finely chopped carrot

½ cup amaretto (optional)

3 tablespoons chili powder

1 tablespoon Worcestershire sauce

4 teaspoons ground cumin

2 teaspoons ground red pepper

1 teaspoon salt

Shredded Cheddar cheese

Combine kidney beans, whole tomatoes, turkey, black beans, tomato sauce, onion, celery, carrot, amaretto, if desired, chili powder, Worcestershire sauce, cumin, ground red pepper and salt in **CROCK-POT®** slow cooker. Cover; cook on HIGH 7 hours. Top each serving with cheese.

Makes 4 servings

Chicken Tortilla Soup

4 boneless, skinless chicken
    thighs
2 cans (about 14 ounces *each*)
    diced tomatoes
1 can (4 ounces) chopped
    mild green chiles, drained
½ to 1 cup chicken broth
1 yellow onion, diced
2 cloves garlic, minced
1 teaspoon ground cumin
    Salt and black pepper
4 corn tortillas, sliced into
    ¼-inch strips
2 tablespoons chopped
    fresh cilantro
½ cup (2 ounces) shredded
    Monterey Jack cheese
1 avocado, diced and tossed
    with lime juice
    Lime wedges

1. Place chicken in **CROCK-POT®** slow cooker. Combine tomatoes, chiles, ½ cup broth, onion, garlic and cumin in small bowl; stir to blend. Pour mixture over chicken. Cover; cook on LOW 6 hours or on HIGH 3 hours.

2. Remove chicken to cutting board. Shred with two forks. Return to cooking liquid. Add salt, pepper and additional broth, if necessary.

3. Just before serving, add tortillas and cilantro to **CROCK-POT®** slow cooker; stir to blend. Top each serving with cheese, avocado and a squeeze of lime juice.

Makes 4 to 6 servings

Turkey-Tomato Soup

2 medium boneless turkey thighs, cut into 1-inch pieces

1¾ cups chicken broth

1½ cups frozen corn, thawed

2 small white or red potatoes, cubed

1 cup chopped onion

1 cup water

1 can (about 8 ounces) tomato sauce

¼ cup tomato paste

2 tablespoons Dijon mustard

1 teaspoon hot pepper sauce

½ teaspoon sugar

½ teaspoon garlic powder

¼ cup finely chopped fresh Italian parsley (optional)

Combine turkey, broth, corn, potatoes, onion, water, tomato sauce, tomato paste, mustard, hot pepper sauce, sugar and garlic powder in **CROCK-POT®** slow cooker. Cover; cook on LOW 9 to 10 hours. Garnish each serving with parsley.

Makes 6 servings

Double Thick Potato-Cheese Soup

2 pounds baking potatoes, cut into ½-inch cubes

2 cans (10½ ounces *each*) condensed cream of mushroom soup

1½ cups finely chopped green onions, divided

¼ teaspoon garlic powder

⅛ teaspoon ground red pepper

1½ cups (6 ounces) shredded sharp Cheddar cheese

1 cup (8 ounces) sour cream

1 cup milk

Black pepper

1. Combine potatoes, soup, 1 cup green onions, garlic powder and ground red pepper in **CROCK-POT®** slow cooker. Cover; cook on LOW 8 hours or on HIGH 4 hours.

2. Stir cheese, sour cream and milk into **CROCK-POT®** slow cooker until cheese is melted. Cover; cook on HIGH 10 minutes. Season with black pepper. Garnish with remaining ½ cup green onions.

Makes 6 servings

Easy Chili

(pictured on page 38)

1 teaspoon vegetable oil

1 pound ground beef

1 medium onion, chopped

2 cans (10¾ ounces *each*) condensed tomato soup, undiluted

1 cup water

Salt and black pepper

Chili powder

Shredded Cheddar cheese (optional)

1. Heat oil in large skillet over medium-high heat. Brown beef and onion 6 to 8 minutes, stirring to break up meat. Remove meat mixture to **CROCK-POT®** slow cooker using slotted spoon.

2. Add soup, water, salt, pepper and chili powder to **CROCK-POT®** slow cooker; stir to blend. Cover; cook on LOW 6 to 8 hours. Sprinkle each serving with cheese, if desired.

Makes 4 servings

Double Thick Potato-Cheese Soup

Chorizo Chili

1 pound ground beef

8 ounces bulk raw chorizo sausage *or* ½ (15-ounce) package raw chorizo sausage, casings removed*

1 can (about 15 ounces) chili beans in chili sauce

2 cans (about 14 ounces *each*) chili-style diced tomatoes

Sour cream and chives (optional)

Shredded Cheddar cheese (optional)

*A highly seasoned Mexican pork sausage.

1. Place beef and chorizo in **CROCK-POT®** slow cooker. Break up with fork to form small pieces. Stir beans and tomatoes into **CROCK-POT®** slow cooker.

2. Cover; cook on LOW 7 hours. Turn off heat. Let stand 10 to 12 minutes. Skim off excess fat from surface. Garnish with sour cream and chives. Serve with cheese, if desired.

Makes 6 servings

Super-Easy Chicken Noodle Soup

1 can (about 48 ounces) chicken broth

2 boneless, skinless chicken breasts, cut into 1-inch pieces

4 cups water

⅔ cup diced onion

⅔ cup diced celery

⅔ cup diced carrots

⅔ cup sliced mushrooms

½ cup frozen peas, thawed

4 cubes chicken bouillon

2 tablespoons butter

1 tablespoon dried parsley flakes

1 teaspoon salt

1 teaspoon ground cumin

1 teaspoon dried marjoram

1 teaspoon black pepper

2 cups cooked egg noodles

French bread (optional)

Combine broth, chicken, water, onion, celery, carrots, mushrooms, peas, bouillon, butter, parsley, salt, cumin, marjoram and pepper in **CROCK-POT**® slow cooker. Cover; cook on LOW 5 to 7 hours or on HIGH 3 to 4 hours. Stir in noodles during last 30 minutes of cooking. Serve with French bread, if desired.

Makes 4 servings

Kick'n Chili

2 pounds ground beef

2 cloves garlic, minced

1 tablespoon *each* salt, ground cumin, chili powder, paprika, dried oregano and black pepper

2 teaspoons red pepper flakes

¼ teaspoon ground red pepper

1 tablespoon vegetable oil

3 cans (about 14 ounces *each*) diced tomatoes with mild green chiles

1 jar (16 ounces) salsa

1 onion, chopped

1. Combine beef, garlic, salt, cumin, chili powder, paprika, oregano, black pepper, red pepper flakes and ground red pepper in large bowl.

2. Heat oil in large skillet over medium-high heat. Brown beef 6 to 8 minutes, stirring to break up meat. Drain fat. Add tomatoes, salsa and onion; mix well.

3. Remove to **CROCK-POT**® slow cooker. Cover; cook on LOW 4 to 6 hours.

Makes 6 servings

 tip

This chunky chili is perfect for the spicy food lover in your family. Reduce the red pepper flakes for a milder flavor.

Roasted Tomato-Basil Soup

2 cans (28 ounces *each*)
    whole tomatoes, drained,
    3 cups liquid reserved

2½ tablespoons packed dark
    brown sugar

1 medium onion, finely
    chopped

3 cups vegetable broth

3 tablespoons tomato paste

¼ teaspoon ground allspice

1 can (5 ounces) evaporated
    milk

¼ cup shredded fresh basil
    (about 10 large leaves)

Salt and black pepper

1. Preheat oven to 450°F. Line baking sheet with foil; spray with nonstick cooking spray. Arrange tomatoes on foil in single layer. Sprinkle with brown sugar; top with onion. Bake 25 minutes or until tomatoes look dry and light brown. Let tomatoes cool slightly; finely chop.

2. Place tomato mixture, 3 cups reserved liquid from tomatoes, broth, tomato paste and allspice in **CROCK-POT®** slow cooker; mix well. Cover; cook on LOW 8 hours or on HIGH 4 hours.

3. Add evaporated milk and basil; season with salt and pepper. Cover; cook on HIGH 30 minutes or until heated through.

Makes 6 servings

Simmered Split Pea Soup

(pictured on page 39)

3 cans (about 14 ounces *each*)
    chicken broth

1 package (16 ounces) dried
    split peas

8 slices bacon, crisp-cooked,
    chopped and divided

1 onion, chopped

2 carrots, chopped

1 teaspoon black pepper

½ teaspoon dried thyme

1 whole bay leaf

Combine broth, peas, half of bacon, onion, carrots, pepper, thyme and bay leaf in **CROCK-POT®** slow cooker. Cover; cook on LOW 6 to 8 hours. Remove and discard bay leaf. Garnish with remaining half of bacon.

Makes 6 servings

Roasted Tomato-Basil Soup

Corn and Two Bean Chili

1 can (about 15 ounces) pinto or kidney beans, rinsed and drained

1 can (about 15 ounces) black beans, rinsed and drained

1 can (about 14 ounces) fire-roasted diced tomatoes

1 cup salsa

1 cup frozen corn, thawed

½ cup minced onion

1 teaspoon chili powder

1 teaspoon ground cumin

½ cup sour cream (optional)

1 cup (4 ounces) shredded Cheddar cheese (optional)

1. Coat inside of **CROCK-POT®** slow cooker with nonstick cooking spray. Combine beans, tomatoes, salsa, corn, onion, chili powder and cumin in **CROCK-POT®** slow cooker; stir to blend.

2. Cover; cook on LOW 5 to 6 hours or on HIGH 2½ to 3 hours. Top each serving with sour cream and cheese, if desired.

Makes 4 servings

Black and White Chili

Nonstick cooking spray

1 pound boneless, skinless chicken breasts, cut into ¾-inch pieces

1 cup chopped onion

1 can (about 15 ounces) Great Northern beans, rinsed and drained

1 can (about 15 ounces) black beans, rinsed and drained

1 can (about 14 ounces) stewed tomatoes, undrained

2 tablespoons Texas-style chili seasoning mix

1. Spray large skillet with cooking spray; heat over medium heat. Add chicken and onion; cook and stir 5 minutes or until chicken is browned.

2. Combine chicken mixture, beans, tomatoes and chili seasoning in **CROCK-POT®** slow cooker. Cover; cook on LOW 4 to 4½ hours.

Makes 6 servings

Serving Suggestion: For a change of pace, this delicious chili is excellent served over cooked rice or pasta.

Potato Soup

(pictured on page 38)

8 slices smoked bacon, divided

1 large onion, chopped

2 stalks celery, chopped

2 carrots, chopped

3 cloves garlic, minced

1 teaspoon dried thyme

5 potatoes (about 3 pounds), cut into ½-inch cubes

4 cups chicken broth

1 cup half-and-half

Salt and black pepper

1. Heat large skillet over medium heat. Add bacon; cook and stir until crisp. Remove to paper towel-lined plate using slotted spoon; crumble.

2. Pour off all but 2 tablespoons bacon fat from skillet; return to medium-high heat. Add onion, celery, carrots, garlic and thyme; cook and stir 6 minutes. Stir onion mixture, potatoes, half of bacon and broth into **CROCK-POT®** slow cooker. Cover; cook on LOW 7 to 8 hours or on HIGH 3 to 4 hours.

3. Mash potatoes with potato masher and stir in half-and-half, salt and pepper. Cover; cook on HIGH 15 minutes. Garnish with remaining half of bacon.

Makes 8 servings

Black and White Chili

Dynamite Chili

½ pound ground beef

Salt and black pepper

2 cans (about 14 ounces *each*)
Italian-style stewed
tomatoes

1 can (about 15 ounces) light
red kidney beans, rinsed
and drained

1 can (about 15 ounces) dark
red kidney beans, rinsed
and drained

1½ cups water

1 large onion, thinly sliced

½ cup chopped red bell pepper

½ cup chopped yellow bell
pepper

2 garlic cloves, minced

2 tablespoons ground chili
powder

1 tablespoon dried parsley
flakes

1 tablespoon ground coriander

1 tablespoon ground cumin

1 teaspoon red pepper flakes

Diced green onions, sour
cream and shredded
Cheddar cheese
(optional)

1. Season beef with salt and pepper. Brown beef in large skillet over medium-high heat 6 to 8 minutes, stirring to break up meat. Drain fat.

2. Add beef, tomatoes, beans, water, onion, bell peppers, garlic, chili powder, parsley, coriander, cumin and red pepper flakes to **CROCK-POT®** slow cooker. Cover; cook on LOW 4 to 6 hours or on HIGH 2 to 3 hours.

Makes 6 servings

Pork Tenderloin Chili

1½ to 2 pounds pork tenderloin, cooked and cut into 2-inch pieces

2 cans (about 15 ounces *each*) pinto beans, rinsed and drained

2 cans (about 15 ounces *each*) black beans, rinsed and drained

2 cans (about 14 ounces *each*) whole tomatoes

2 cans (4 ounces *each*) diced mild green chiles

1 package taco seasoning mix

Optional toppings: diced avocado, shredded cheese, chopped onion, cilantro and/or tortilla chips

Combine pork, beans, tomatoes, chiles and taco seasoning mix in **CROCK-POT®** slow cooker. Cover; cook on LOW 4 hours. Top as desired.

Makes 8 servings

Broccoli Rabe and Sausage Rigatoni (page 100)

Turkey Stroganoff (page 99)

Pasta Dinners

Beefy Tortellini (page 98)

Three-Pepper Pasta Sauce

1 *each* red, yellow and green
　　bell pepper, cut into
　　1-inch pieces

2 cans (about 14 ounces *each*)
　　diced tomatoes

1 cup chopped onion

1 can (6 ounces) tomato paste

4 cloves garlic, minced

2 tablespoons olive oil

1 teaspoon dried basil

1 teaspoon dried oregano

½ teaspoon salt

¼ teaspoon red pepper flakes
　　or black pepper

　Hot cooked pasta

　Grated Parmesan or Romano
　　cheese

Combine bell peppers, tomatoes, onion, tomato paste, garlic, oil, basil, oregano, salt and red pepper flakes in **CROCK-POT®** slow cooker. Cover; cook on LOW 7 to 8 hours. Serve with pasta and cheese.

Makes 4 to 6 servings

tip

Save preparation time! Substitute 3 cups of mixed bell pepper pieces from a salad bar for the bell peppers.

Spaghetti and Turkey Meatballs

1½ pounds ground turkey

½ cup seasoned dry bread
  crumbs

1 small onion, finely chopped

2 teaspoons garlic powder,
  divided

2 eggs

½ cup grated Parmesan
  cheese

½ teaspoon black pepper,
  divided

2 tablespoons olive oil

1 can (28 ounces) crushed
  tomatoes with basil,
  oregano and garlic

1 can (6 ounces) tomato paste

1 teaspoon dried basil

  Hot cooked spaghetti

  Chopped fresh Italian
  parsley (optional)

1. Coat inside of **CROCK-POT®** slow cooker with nonstick cooking spray. Combine turkey, bread crumbs, onion, 1 teaspoon garlic powder, eggs, cheese and ¼ teaspoon pepper in large bowl; mix well. Form mixture into 24 meatballs, about 1½ inches in diameter.

2. Heat oil in large skillet over medium-high heat. Add meatballs in batches; cook and stir 4 to 5 minutes or until browned on all sides. Remove meatballs to **CROCK-POT®** slow cooker using slotted spoon.

3. Combine tomatoes, tomato paste and basil in large bowl; stir to blend. Pour over meatballs. Cover; cook on LOW 6 to 7 hours or on HIGH 3 to 4 hours. Serve over spaghetti. Garnish with parsley.

Makes 6 servings

Artichoke Pasta

1 tablespoon olive oil

1 cup chopped sweet onion

4 cloves garlic, minced

1 can (28 ounces) crushed
    tomatoes

1 can (about 14 ounces)
    artichoke hearts, drained
    and cut into pieces

1 cup small pimiento-stuffed
    olives

¾ teaspoon red pepper flakes

8 ounces hot cooked
    fettuccine pasta

½ cup grated Asiago or
    Romano cheese

Fresh basil (optional)

1. Coat inside of **CROCK-POT**® slow cooker with nonstick cooking spray. Heat oil in small skillet over medium heat. Add onion; cook and stir 5 minutes. Add garlic; cook and stir 1 minute. Combine onion mixture, tomatoes, artichokes, olives and red pepper flakes in **CROCK-POT**® slow cooker.

2. Cover; cook on LOW 7 to 8 hours or on HIGH 3 to 4 hours. Top pasta with artichoke sauce and cheese. Garnish with basil.

Makes 4 servings

Stuffed Manicotti

1 container (15 ounces) ricotta
    cheese
1½ cups (6 ounces) shredded
    Italian cheese blend,
    divided
1 egg
¼ teaspoon ground nutmeg
10 uncooked manicotti shells
2 cans (about 14 ounces *each*)
    Italian seasoned stewed
    tomatoes
1 cup spicy marinara or
    tomato basil pasta sauce
Chopped fresh basil or
    Italian parsley (optional)
French bread (optional)

1. Combine ricotta cheese, 1 cup Italian cheese, egg and nutmeg in medium bowl; mix well. Spoon mixture into large resealable food storage bag; cut off small corner. Pipe cheese mixture into uncooked manicotti shells.

2. Coat inside of **CROCK-POT®** slow cooker with nonstick cooking spray. Combine tomatoes and pasta sauce in large bowl; stir until blended. Spoon 1½ cups sauce mixture into **CROCK-POT®** slow cooker. Arrange half of the stuffed shells in sauce. Repeat layering with 1½ cups sauce, remaining shells and remaining sauce. Cover; cook on LOW 2½ to 3 hours.

3. Sprinkle remaining ½ cup Italian cheese over top. Turn **CROCK-POT®** slow cooker to HIGH. Cover; cook on HIGH 10 to 15 minutes or until cheese is melted. Garnish with basil. Serve with bread, if desired.

Makes 5 servings

Garden Pasta

1 jar (24 to 26 ounces)
    puttanesca or spicy
    tomato basil pasta sauce

1 can (about 14 ounces)
    stewed tomatoes

1 cup small broccoli florets

1 cup finely diced yellow
    squash or zucchini *or*
    ½ cup *each*

½ cup water

2 cups (5 ounces) uncooked
    bowtie pasta

½ cup crumbled feta cheese

¼ cup chopped fresh basil

1. Coat inside of **CROCK-POT®** slow cooker with nonstick cooking spray. Combine pasta sauce, tomatoes, broccoli, squash, water and pasta in **CROCK-POT®** slow cooker; mix well.

2. Cover; cook on LOW 3½ to 4½ hours or on HIGH 2 to 2½ hours, stirring halfway through cooking time. Spoon into shallow bowls; top with cheese and basil.

Makes 4 to 6 servings

Pasta Shells with Prosciutto

3 cups (8 ounces) uncooked
    medium shell pasta

1 jar (24 to 26 ounces) vodka
    pasta sauce

¾ cup water

½ cup whipping cream

2 ounces (½ cup) torn or
    coarsely chopped thin
    sliced prosciutto

¼ cup chopped fresh chives

1. Coat inside of **CROCK-POT®** slow cooker with nonstick cooking spray. Combine pasta, pasta sauce and water in **CROCK-POT®** slow cooker. Cover; cook on LOW 2 hours or on HIGH 1 hour.

2. Stir in cream. Cover; cook on LOW 1 to 1½ hours or on HIGH 45 minutes to 1 hour or until pasta is tender.

3. Stir prosciutto into pasta mixture. Spoon into shallow bowls; top with chives.

Makes 4 servings

Easy Parmesan Chicken

8 ounces mushrooms, sliced

1 medium onion, cut into thin wedges

1 tablespoon olive oil

4 boneless, skinless chicken breasts

1 jar (26 ounces) pasta sauce

½ teaspoon dried basil

¼ teaspoon dried oregano

1 whole bay leaf

½ cup (2 ounces) shredded mozzarella cheese

¼ cup grated Parmesan cheese

Hot cooked spaghetti

1. Place mushrooms and onion in **CROCK-POT®** slow cooker.

2. Heat oil in large skillet over medium-high heat. Add chicken; cook 3 to 5 minutes on each side or until lightly browned. Place chicken in **CROCK-POT®** slow cooker. Pour pasta sauce over chicken; add basil, oregano and bay leaf. Cover; cook on LOW 6 to 7 hours or on HIGH 3 to 4 hours. Remove and discard bay leaf.

3. Sprinkle chicken with cheeses. Cook, uncovered, on LOW 10 minutes or until cheeses are melted. Serve over spaghetti.

Makes 4 servings

tip

Dairy products should be added at the end of the cooking time because they will curdle if cooked in the **CROCK-POT®** slow cooker for a long time.

Vegetable Pasta Sauce

2 cans (about 14 ounces *each*)
    diced tomatoes

1 can (about 14 ounces) whole
    tomatoes, undrained

1½ cups sliced mushrooms

1 medium red bell pepper,
    diced

1 medium green bell pepper,
    diced

1 small yellow squash, cut into
    ¼-inch slices

1 small zucchini, cut into
    ¼-inch slices

1 can (6 ounces) tomato paste

4 green onions, sliced

2 tablespoons Italian
    seasoning

1 tablespoon chopped fresh
    Italian parsley

3 cloves garlic, minced

1 teaspoon salt

1 teaspoon red pepper flakes
    (optional)

1 teaspoon black pepper

    Hot cooked rigatoni pasta

    Grated Parmesan cheese
    (optional)

Combine tomatoes, mushrooms, bell peppers, squash, zucchini, tomato paste, green onions, Italian seasoning, parsley, garlic, salt, red pepper flakes, if desired, and black pepper in **CROCK-POT®** slow cooker; stir until well blended. Cover; cook on LOW 6 to 8 hours. Serve over pasta. Top with cheese, if desired.

Makes 4 to 6 servings

Cream Cheese Chicken with Broccoli

4 pounds boneless, skinless chicken breasts, cut into ½-inch pieces

1 tablespoon olive oil

1 package (1 ounce) Italian salad dressing mix

Nonstick cooking spray

2 cups (about 8 ounces) sliced mushrooms

1 cup chopped onion

1 can (10½ ounces) condensed cream of chicken soup, undiluted

1 bag (10 ounces) frozen broccoli florets, thawed

1 package (8 ounces) cream cheese, cubed

¼ cup dry sherry

Hot cooked pasta

1. Toss chicken with oil in large bowl. Sprinkle with salad dressing mix. Remove to **CROCK-POT**® slow cooker. Cover; cook on LOW 3 hours.

2. Spray large skillet with cooking spray; heat over medium heat. Add mushrooms and onion; cook 5 minutes or until onion is tender.

3. Add soup, broccoli, cream cheese and sherry to skillet; cook and stir until heated through. Remove to **CROCK-POT**® slow cooker. Cover; cook on LOW 1 hour. Serve chicken and sauce over pasta.

Makes 10 to 12 servings

tip

For easier preparation, cut up the chicken and vegetables for this recipe the night before. Wrap the chicken and vegetables separately, and store in the refrigerator.

Greek Chicken Ragoût

1 pound small red potatoes

1 pound baby carrots

2 red bell peppers, sliced

1 onion, chopped

2 cloves garlic, finely chopped

1 can (about 14 ounces) chicken broth

10 skinless chicken thighs

1 teaspoon salt

1 teaspoon dried oregano, divided

1 teaspoon dried marjoram, divided

¼ teaspoon black pepper

1 package (9 ounces) frozen artichoke hearts, thawed

2 teaspoons grated lemon peel

1 tablespoon lemon juice

1 tablespoon tomato paste

¼ cup water

3 tablespoons cornstarch

8 ounces feta cheese

5 cups hot cooked orzo pasta

1. Combine potatoes, carrots, bell peppers, onion, garlic and broth in **CROCK-POT®** slow cooker. Add chicken; season with salt, ½ teaspoon oregano, ½ teaspoon marjoram and black pepper. Cover; cook on LOW 8 to 10 hours or on HIGH 3½ hours.

2. Top with artichoke hearts. Cover; cook on HIGH 30 to 45 minutes or until chicken is cooked through and artichoke hearts are heated through. Remove chicken and vegetables to serving bowl using slotted spoon.

3. Whisk lemon peel, lemon juice and tomato paste into cooking liquid in **CROCK-POT®** slow cooker. Stir water into cornstarch in small bowl until smooth; whisk into **CROCK-POT®** slow cooker. Cover; cook on HIGH 10 minutes or until sauce is thickened. Pour over chicken and vegetables; top with feta. Serve over orzo.

Makes 10 servings

Pantry Beef Stroganoff

3 tablespoons all-purpose
  flour, divided

1½ teaspoons dried thyme

½ teaspoon black pepper

1 pound cubed beef stew meat

1 tablespoon vegetable or
  olive oil

1 can (10¾ ounces) condensed
  cream of mushroom soup

½ cup beef broth

½ cup chopped onion

¾ cup sour cream

3 cups hot cooked egg
  noodles

Minced fresh Italian parsley
  (optional)

1. Place 2 tablespoons flour, thyme, pepper and beef in large resealable storage bag; shake to coat. Heat oil in large skillet over medium heat. Add half of meat; cook 4 to 5 minutes or until browned on all sides, turning occasionally.

2. Coat inside of **CROCK-POT**® slow cooker with nonstick cooking spray. Add soup and broth; mix well. Add browned meat. Brown remaining half of meat with onion in same skillet; add to **CROCK-POT**® slow cooker and mix well.

3. Cover; cook on LOW 6 to 7 hours or on HIGH 3 to 4 hours. Whisk remaining 1 tablespoon flour into sour cream in medium bowl. Whisk in ¼ cup of liquid from **CROCK-POT**® slow cooker; return mixture to **CROCK-POT**® slow cooker; mix well. Cover; cook on HIGH 10 minutes or until sauce is thickened. Serve over noodles. Garnish with parsley.

Makes 4 servings

Beefy Tortellini

(pictured on page 75)

½ pound ground beef

1 jar (24 to 26 ounces) roasted tomato and garlic pasta sauce

½ cup water

8 ounces sliced button or exotic mushrooms, such as oyster, shiitake and cremini

½ teaspoon red pepper flakes (optional)

1 package (12 ounces) uncooked three-cheese tortellini

¾ cup grated Asiago or Romano cheese

Chopped fresh Italian parsley (optional)

1. Brown beef in large skillet over medium-high heat 6 to 8 minutes, stirring to break up meat. Drain fat.

2. Coat inside of **CROCK-POT**® slow cooker with nonstick cooking spray. Stir pasta sauce and water into **CROCK-POT**® slow cooker. Add mushrooms; stir to combine. Stir in meat, red pepper flakes, if desired, and tortellini. Cover; cook on LOW 2 hours or on HIGH 1 hour. Stir.

3. Cover; cook on LOW 2 to 2½ hours or on HIGH ½ to 1 hour. Serve in shallow bowls topped with cheese and parsley, if desired.

Makes 6 servings

Turkey Stroganoff

(pictured on page 74)

Nonstick cooking spray

4 cups sliced mushrooms

2 stalks celery, thinly sliced

2 medium shallots *or* **½ small onion, minced**

1 cup chicken broth

½ teaspoon dried thyme

¼ teaspoon black pepper

2 turkey tenderloins, turkey breasts *or* **boneless, skinless chicken thighs (about 10 ounces** *each***), cut into 1-inch pieces**

½ cup sour cream

1 tablespoon plus 1 teaspoon all-purpose flour

¼ teaspoon salt

1⅓ cups hot cooked wide egg noodles

1. Spray large skillet with nonstick cooking spray; heat over medium heat. Add mushrooms, celery and shallots; cook and stir 5 minutes or until mushrooms and shallot are tender. Spoon into **CROCK-POT®** slow cooker. Stir broth, thyme and pepper into **CROCK-POT®** slow cooker. Stir in turkey. Cover; cook on LOW 5 to 6 hours.

2. Mix sour cream into flour in small bowl. Spoon 2 tablespoons liquid from **CROCK-POT®** slow cooker into sour cream mixture; stir well. Stir sour cream mixture into **CROCK-POT®** slow cooker. Cover; cook on LOW 10 minutes.

3. Season with salt. Spoon noodles onto each plate to serve. Top with turkey mixture.

Makes 4 servings

Ham and Cheese Pasta Bake

12 ounces uncooked rigatoni
pasta

1 ham steak, cubed

1 container (10 ounces)
refrigerated Alfredo
sauce

2 cups (8 ounces) shredded
mozzarella cheese,
divided

2 cups half-and-half, warmed

1 tablespoon cornstarch

1. Fill large saucepan with salted water; bring to a boil over high heat. Add pasta; cook 7 minutes. Drain pasta; remove to **CROCK-POT**® slow cooker.

2. Stir ham, Alfredo sauce and 1 cup cheese into pasta. Stir half-and-half into cornstarch in medium bowl until smooth; pour over pasta. Sprinkle with remaining 1 cup cheese. Cover; cook on LOW 3½ to 4 hours or until pasta is tender and liquid is absorbed.

Makes 6 servings

Broccoli Rabe and Sausage Rigatoni

(pictured on page 74)

2 tablespoons olive oil

3 sweet or hot Italian sausage
links, casings removed

2 cloves garlic, minced

1 large bunch (about
1¼ pounds) broccoli rabe,
trimmed and cut into
1-inch lengths

½ cup chicken broth

½ teaspoon salt

½ teaspoon red pepper flakes

1 pound hot cooked rigatoni
pasta

Grated Parmesan cheese
(optional)

1. Coat inside of **CROCK-POT**® slow cooker with nonstick cooking spray. Heat oil in large skillet over medium heat. Add sausage; cook and stir 6 to 8 minutes or until browned. Add garlic; cook and stir 1 minute or until softened and fragrant. Remove to **CROCK-POT**® slow cooker using slotted spoon.

2. Add broccoli rabe to **CROCK-POT**® slow cooker with sausage. Pour in broth; season with salt and red pepper flakes. Cover; cook on LOW 4 hours or on HIGH 2 hours.

3. Stir pasta into sausage mixture in **CROCK-POT**® slow cooker just before serving. Garnish with cheese.

Makes 6 servings

Ham and Cheese Pasta Bake

Pizza-Style Mostaccioli

1 jar (24 to 26 ounces)
   marinara sauce or tomato
   basil pasta sauce

½ cup water

2 cups (6 ounces) uncooked
   mostaccioli pasta

1 package (8 ounces) sliced
   mushrooms

1 small yellow or green bell
   pepper, finely diced

½ cup (1 ounce) sliced
   pepperoni, halved

1 teaspoon dried oregano

¼ teaspoon red pepper flakes

1 cup (4 ounces) shredded
   pizza cheese blend or
   Italian cheese blend

Chopped fresh oregano
   (optional)

Garlic bread (optional)

1. Coat inside of **CROCK-POT**® slow cooker with nonstick cooking spray. Combine marinara sauce and water in **CROCK-POT**® slow cooker. Stir in pasta, mushrooms, bell pepper, pepperoni, dried oregano and red pepper flakes; mix well. Cover; cook on LOW 2 hours or on HIGH 1 hour.

2. Stir well. Cover; cook on LOW 1½ to 2 hours or on HIGH 45 minutes to 1 hour.* Spoon into shallow bowls. Top with cheese and garnish with fresh oregano. Serve with bread, if desired.

Stirring halfway through cooking time prevents the pasta on the bottom from becoming overcooked.

Makes 4 servings

Broccoli and Beef Pasta

2 cups broccoli florets *or*
  1 package (10 ounces)
  frozen broccoli, thawed

1 onion, thinly sliced

½ teaspoon dried basil

½ teaspoon dried oregano

½ teaspoon dried thyme

1 can (about 14 ounces)
  Italian-style diced
  tomatoes

¾ cup beef broth

1 pound ground beef

2 cloves garlic, minced

2 cups hot cooked rotini pasta

¾ cup grated Parmesan
  cheese, plus additional
  for garnish

2 tablespoons tomato paste

1. Layer broccoli, onion, basil, oregano, thyme, tomatoes and broth in **CROCK-POT®** slow cooker. Cover; cook on LOW 2½ hours.

2. Cook beef and garlic in large nonstick skillet over medium-high heat 6 to 8 minutes, stirring to break up meat. Remove to **CROCK-POT®** slow cooker using slotted spoon. Cover; cook on LOW 2 hours.

3. Stir in pasta, ¾ cup cheese and tomato paste. Cover; cook on LOW 30 minutes or until cheese is melted and mixture is heated through. Sprinkle with additional cheese.

Makes 4 servings

Serving Suggestion: Serve with garlic bread.

Thai Turkey and Noodles

1 package (about 1½ pounds)
    turkey tenderloins, cut
    into ¾-inch pieces

1 red bell pepper, cut into
    short, thin strips

1¼ cups chicken broth, divided

¼ cup soy sauce

3 cloves garlic, minced

¾ teaspoon red pepper flakes

¼ teaspoon salt

2 tablespoons cornstarch

3 green onions, cut into
    ½-inch pieces

⅓ cup creamy or chunky
    peanut butter (not
    natural-style)

12 ounces hot cooked
    vermicelli pasta

¾ cup peanuts or cashews,
    chopped

¾ cup fresh cilantro, chopped

    Sprigs fresh cilantro
    (optional)

1. Place turkey, bell pepper, 1 cup broth, soy sauce, garlic, red pepper flakes and salt in **CROCK-POT**® slow cooker. Cover; cook on LOW 3 to 4 hours.

2. Stir remaining ¼ cup broth and cornstarch in small bowl until smooth. Stir green onions, peanut butter and cornstarch mixture into **CROCK-POT**® slow cooker. Turn **CROCK-POT**® slow cooker to HIGH. Cover; cook on HIGH 30 minutes or until sauce is thickened. Stir well.

3. Serve over pasta. Sprinkle with peanuts and cilantro.

Makes 8 servings

Variation: Substitute ramen noodles for vermicelli. Discard the flavor packet from ramen soup mix and drop the noodles into boiling water. Cook the noodles 2 to 3 minutes or until just tender. Drain and top with turkey mixture.

Cheesy Slow Cooker Chicken

6 boneless, skinless chicken breasts (about 1½ pounds)

Salt and black pepper

Garlic powder

2 cans (10½ ounces *each*) condensed cream of chicken soup, undiluted

1 can (10½ ounces) condensed Cheddar cheese soup, undiluted

Hot cooked pasta

Chopped fresh Italian parsley (optional)

1. Place 3 chicken breasts in **CROCK-POT®** slow cooker. Season with salt, pepper and garlic powder. Repeat with remaining 3 breasts and seasonings.

2. Combine soups in medium bowl; pour over chicken. Cover; cook on LOW 6 to 8 hours. Serve over pasta. Garnish with parsley.

Makes 6 servings

Note: This sauce is also delicious over rice or mashed potatoes.

CROCK·POT
◆ THE ORIGINAL SLOW COOKER ◆

Southwestern Mac and Cheese (page 118)

Chicken and Biscuits (page 114)

6 Ingredients or Less

So Simple Supper! (page 120)

BBQ Turkey Legs

BBQ Sauce (recipe follows)
6 turkey drumsticks
2 teaspoons salt
2 teaspoons black pepper

1. Prepare BBQ Sauce.

2. Season drumsticks with salt and pepper. Place in **CROCK-POT®** slow cooker. Add BBQ Sauce; turn to coat. Cover; cook on LOW 7 to 8 hours or on HIGH 3 to 4 hours.

Makes 6 servings

BBQ Sauce

½ cup white vinegar
½ cup ketchup
½ cup molasses
¼ cup Worcestershire sauce
1 tablespoon onion powder
1 tablespoon garlic powder
1 teaspoon hickory liquid smoke
⅛ teaspoon chipotle chili pepper

Combine vinegar, ketchup, molasses, Worcestershire sauce, onion powder, garlic powder, liquid smoke and chipotle chili pepper in large bowl; stir to blend.

Makes about 2 cups

Super-Easy Beef Burritos

1 boneless beef chuck roast
(2 to 3 pounds)*

1 can (28 ounces) enchilada
sauce

2 to 3 tablespoons water
(optional)

4 (8-inch) flour tortillas

*Unless you have a 5-, 6- or 7-quart
CROCK-POT® slow cooker, cut any
roast larger than 2½ pounds in half so
it cooks completely.

1. Place roast in **CROCK-POT**® slow cooker; cover with enchilada sauce. Add water, if desired. Cover; cook on LOW 6 to 8 hours.

2. Remove beef to cutting board; shred with two forks. Serve in tortillas.

Makes 4 servings

Serving Suggestion: Excellent garnishes include shredded cheese, sour cream, salsa, lettuce and tomatoes.

Chicken and Biscuits

(pictured on page 110)

4 boneless, skinless chicken
breasts, cut into 1-inch
pieces

1 can (10¾ ounces) condensed
cream of chicken soup

1 package (10 ounces) frozen
peas and carrots, thawed

1 package (7½ ounces)
refrigerated biscuits

1. Place chicken in **CROCK-POT**® slow cooker; pour in soup. Cover; cook on LOW 4 hours.

2. Stir in peas and carrots. Cover; cook on LOW 30 minutes or until vegetables are heated through.

3. Meanwhile, bake biscuits according to package directions. Spoon chicken and vegetable mixture over biscuits to serve.

Makes 4 servings

Super-Easy Beef Burritos

Crock and Go Ham with Pineapple Glaze

1 (3- to 5-pound) ham

10 to 12 whole cloves

1 can (8 ounces) sliced pineapple, juice reserved and divided

2 tablespoons packed brown sugar

1 jar (4 ounces) maraschino cherries plus 1 tablespoon juice reserved and divided

1. Stud ham with cloves. Place ham in **CROCK-POT®** slow cooker.

2. Combine reserved pineapple juice, brown sugar and reserved 1 tablespoon cherry juice in medium bowl; stir until glaze forms. Pour glaze over ham in **CROCK-POT®** slow cooker. Arrange sliced pineapple and cherries over ham. Cover; cook on LOW 6 to 8 hours. Remove cloves before serving.

Makes 6 to 8 servings

BBQ Pulled Chicken Sandwiches

1¼ to 1½ pounds boneless, skinless chicken thighs

¾ cup barbecue sauce, divided

1 package (14 ounces) frozen bell pepper and onion strips cut for stir-fry, thawed and well drained

¼ to ½ teaspoon hot pepper sauce

4 Kaiser rolls, split and toasted

1. Combine chicken and ¼ cup barbecue sauce in **CROCK-POT®** slow cooker; mix well. Add bell pepper and onion strips; mix well. Cover; cook on LOW 5 to 6 hours or on HIGH 2 to 3 hours.

2. Remove chicken to medium bowl; use two forks to shred chicken. Drain pepper mixture; add to bowl with chicken. Add remaining ½ cup barbecue sauce and hot pepper sauce; mix well. Serve in rolls.

Makes 4 servings

Crock and Go Ham with Pineapple Glaze

Simply Delicious Pork Roast

1½ pounds boneless pork loin,
cut into 6 pieces *or*
6 boneless pork loin
chops
4 medium Golden Delicious
apples, peeled and sliced
3 tablespoons packed brown
sugar
1 teaspoon ground cinnamon
½ teaspoon salt

1. Place pork in **CROCK-POT®** slow cooker. Cover with apples.

2. Combine brown sugar, cinnamon and salt in small bowl; sprinkle over apples. Cover; cook on LOW 6 to 8 hours.

Makes 6 servings

Southwestern Mac and Cheese

(pictured on page 110)

1 package (8 ounces)
uncooked elbow
macaroni
1 can (about 14 ounces) diced
tomatoes with green
peppers and onions
1 can (10 ounces) diced
tomatoes with mild green
chiles
1½ cups salsa
3 cups (12 ounces) shredded
Mexican cheese blend,
divided

1. Coat inside of **CROCK-POT®** slow cooker with nonstick cooking spray. Layer macaroni, tomatoes, salsa and 2 cups cheese in **CROCK-POT®** slow cooker. Cover; cook on LOW 3¾ hours.

2. Sprinkle remaining 1 cup cheese over macaroni. Cover; cook on LOW 15 minutes or until cheese is melted.

Makes 6 servings

Simply Delicious Pork Roast

Chicken Scaloppine in Alfredo Sauce

2 tablespoons all-purpose flour

Salt and black pepper

1 pound boneless, skinless chicken tenderloins, cut lengthwise in half

1 tablespoon butter

1 tablespoon olive oil

1 cup Alfredo pasta sauce

1 package (12 ounces) spinach noodles, cooked and drained

1. Place flour, salt and pepper in large bowl. Add chicken; toss to coat. Heat butter and oil in large skillet over medium-high heat. Add chicken; cook 3 minutes per side or until browned. Remove chicken in single layer to **CROCK-POT**® slow cooker.

2. Add Alfredo pasta sauce to **CROCK-POT**® slow cooker. Cover; cook on LOW 1 to 1½ hours. Spoon chicken and sauce over noodles.

Makes 6 servings

So Simple Supper!

(pictured on page 111)

1 boneless beef chuck shoulder roast (3 to 4 pounds)*

3 cups water

1 package (about 1 ounce) dry onion soup mix

1 package (about 1 ounce) au jus gravy mix

1 package (about 1 ounce) mushroom gravy mix

Assorted vegetables (potatoes, carrots, onions and celery)

1. Place beef in **CROCK-POT**® slow cooker. Combine water, soup mix and gravy mixes in large bowl. Pour gravy mixture over beef in **CROCK-POT**® slow cooker. Cover; cook on LOW 4 hours.

2. Add vegetables. Cover; cook on LOW 4 hours.

Makes 8 servings

*Unless you have a 5-, 6- or 7-quart **CROCK-POT**® *slow cooker, cut any roast larger than 2½ pounds in half so it cooks completely.*

Chicken Scaloppine in Alfredo Sauce

Root Beer BBQ Pulled Pork

1 can (12 ounces) root beer
1 bottle (18 ounces) sweet
    barbecue sauce, divided
1 package (1 ounce) dry onion
    soup mix
1 (6- to 8-pound) boneless
    pork shoulder roast
Salt and black pepper
Hamburger buns

1. Combine root beer and ½ bottle barbecue sauce in **CROCK-POT®** slow cooker. Rub soup mix on pork roast; place in **CROCK-POT®** slow cooker. Cover; cook on LOW 8 to 10 hours.

2. Remove pork to cutting board; shred with two forks. Reserve 1 cup barbecue mixture in **CROCK-POT®** slow cooker; discard remaining mixture. Turn **CROCK-POT®** slow cooker to HIGH. Stir shredded pork and remaining ½ bottle barbecue sauce, salt and pepper into **CROCK-POT®** slow cooker. Cover; cook on HIGH 20 minutes or until heated through. Serve on buns.

Makes 8 servings

Brisket with Sweet Onions

2 large sweet onions, cut into
    10 (½-inch) slices*
1 flat-cut boneless beef
    brisket (about 3½ pounds)
Salt and black pepper
2 cans (about 14 ounces *each*)
    beef broth
1 teaspoon cracked black
    peppercorns

Preferably Maui, Vidalia or Walla Walla onions.

1. Coat inside of **CROCK-POT®** slow cooker with nonstick cooking spray. Line bottom with onion slices.

2. Season brisket with salt and pepper. Heat large skillet over medium-high heat. Add brisket; cook 10 to 12 minutes or until browned on all sides. Remove to **CROCK-POT®** slow cooker.

3. Pour broth into **CROCK-POT®** slow cooker. Sprinkle brisket with peppercorns. Cover; cook on HIGH 5 to 7 hours.

4. Remove brisket to cutting board. Cover loosely with foil; let stand 10 to 15 minutes. Slice against the grain into ¾-inch slices. Serve with cooking liquid.

Makes 10 servings

Root Beer BBQ Pulled Pork

Corned Beef and Cabbage

1 head cabbage (about 1½ pounds), cut into 6 wedges

4 ounces baby carrots

1 corned beef (about 3 pounds), with seasoning packet (perforate packet with knife tip)

4 cups water

⅓ cup prepared mustard

⅓ cup honey

1. Place cabbage and carrots in **CROCK-POT®** slow cooker. Place seasoning packet on top. Add corned beef, fat side up. Pour in water. Cover; cook on LOW 10 hours.

2. Remove and discard seasoning packet. Combine mustard and honey in small bowl. Slice beef; serve with vegetables and mustard sauce.

Makes 6 servings

tip

To make clean up easier, coat the inside of the **CROCK-POT®** slow cooker with nonstick cooking spray before adding ingredients.

Slow Cooker Turkey Breast

½ to 1 teaspoon garlic powder

½ to 1 teaspoon paprika

1 turkey breast (4 to 6 pounds)

1 tablespoon dried parsley
flakes

1. Combine garlic powder and paprika in small bowl; rub onto turkey. Place turkey in **CROCK-POT®** slow cooker. Sprinkle with parsley. Cover; cook on LOW 6 to 8 hours or on HIGH 2½ to 3 hours.

2. Remove turkey to cutting board. Cover loosely with foil; let stand 10 to 15 minutes before slicing.

Makes 4 to 6 servings

No-Fuss Macaroni and Cheese

2 cups (about 8 ounces)
uncooked elbow
macaroni

4 ounces pasteurized process
cheese product, cut into
cubes

1 cup (4 ounces) shredded
mild Cheddar cheese

½ teaspoon salt

⅛ teaspoon black pepper

1½ cups milk

Combine macaroni, cheese product, Cheddar cheese, salt and pepper in **CROCK-POT®** slow cooker. Pour in milk. Cover; cook on LOW 2 to 3 hours, stirring after 20 to 30 minutes.

Makes 6 to 8 servings

Slow Cooker Turkey Breast

Easy Beef Sandwiches

1 large onion, sliced

1 boneless beef bottom
round roast (about 3 to
5 pounds)*

1 cup water

1 package (about 1 ounce)
au jus gravy mix

French rolls, sliced
lengthwise

Provolone cheese

*Unless you have a 5-, 6- or 7-quart
CROCK-POT® slow cooker, cut any
roast larger than 2½ pounds in half so
it cooks completely.

1. Place onion slices in bottom of **CROCK-POT**®
slow cooker; top with roast. Combine water and
gravy mix in small bowl; pour over roast. Cover;
cook on LOW 7 to 9 hours.

2. Remove roast to cutting board. Shred meat using
two forks. Serve on rolls; top with cheese. Serve
cooking liquid on the side for dipping.

Makes 6 to 8 servings

tip

For additional flavor, brown the
beef roast in a large skillet before
adding to the **CROCK-POT**® slow
cooker.

Harvest Ham Supper

6 carrots, cut into 2-inch
   pieces
3 medium sweet potatoes,
   quartered
1 to 1½ pounds boneless ham
1 cup maple syrup

1. Arrange carrots and sweet potatoes in bottom of
CROCK-POT® slow cooker.

2. Place ham on top of vegetables. Pour syrup over
ham and vegetables. Cover; cook on LOW 6 to
8 hours.

Makes 6 servings

Slow Cooker Chicken Dinner

4 boneless, skinless chicken
   breasts (about 1 pound)
1 can (10½ ounces) condensed
   cream of chicken soup,
   undiluted
⅓ cup milk
1 package (6 ounces) stuffing
   mix
1⅔ cups water

1. Place chicken in **CROCK-POT®** slow cooker.
Combine soup and milk in small bowl. Pour soup
mixture over chicken.

2. Combine stuffing mix and water in large bowl.
Spoon stuffing over chicken. Cover; cook on
LOW 6 to 8 hours.

Makes 4 servings

Harvest Ham Supper

CROCK·POT®

·THE ORIGINAL SLOW COOKER·

Easy Family Burritos (page 154)

Cinnamon Roll and Sweet
'Tater Gratin (page 143)

Kids Favorites

Super Meatball Sliders (page 142)

Pulled Pork Sliders with Cola Barbecue Sauce

1 teaspoon vegetable oil

3 pounds boneless pork shoulder roast, cut evenly into 4 pieces

1 cup cola

¼ cup tomato paste

2 tablespoons packed brown sugar

2 teaspoons Worcestershire sauce

2 teaspoons spicy brown mustard

Hot pepper sauce

Salt

16 dinner rolls or potato rolls, split

Sliced pickles (optional)

1. Heat oil in large skillet over medium-high heat. Brown pork on all sides. Remove to **CROCK-POT®** slow cooker. Pour cola over pork. Cover; cook on LOW 7½ to 8 hours or on HIGH 3½ to 4 hours.

2. Remove pork to cutting board. Cover loosely with foil; let stand 10 to 15 minutes. Shred pork with two forks.

3. Skim fat from cooking liquid. Whisk tomato paste, brown sugar, Worcestershire sauce and mustard into **CROCK-POT®** slow cooker. Cover; cook on HIGH 15 minutes or until thickened.

4. Stir shredded pork into **CROCK-POT®** slow cooker. Season with hot pepper sauce and salt. Serve on rolls. Top with pickles, if desired.

Makes 16 sliders

Southwest-Style Meat Loaf

1½ pounds ground beef

2 eggs

1 small onion, chopped
(about ½ cup)

½ medium green bell pepper,
chopped (about ½ cup)

½ cup plain dry bread crumbs

¾ cup chunky salsa, divided

1½ teaspoons ground cumin

¾ cup (3 ounces) shredded
Mexican cheese blend

¾ teaspoon salt

¼ teaspoon black pepper

1. Combine beef, eggs, onion, bell pepper, bread crumbs, ¼ cup salsa, cumin, cheese, salt and black pepper in large bowl; mix well. Form mixture into 9×5-inch loaf.

2. Fold two long pieces of foil in half lengthwise. (Each should be about 24 inches long.) Crisscross pieces on work surface, coat with nonstick cooking spray and set meat loaf on top. Use ends of foil as handles to gently lower meat loaf into **CROCK-POT®** slow cooker, letting ends hang over the top. Top meat loaf with remaining ½ cup salsa.

3. Cover; cook on LOW 7 to 8 hours or on HIGH 3 to 4 hours or until meat loaf is firm and cooked through. Remove meat loaf to cutting board; let stand 5 minutes before slicing.

Makes 6 servings

Tuna Casserole

2 cans (10¾ ounces *each*)
    cream of celery soup

2 cans (5 ounces *each*) tuna in
    water, drained and flaked

1 cup water

2 carrots, chopped

1 small red onion, chopped

¼ teaspoon black pepper

1 egg

8 ounces hot cooked egg
    noodles

Plain dry bread crumbs

2 tablespoons chopped fresh
    Italian parsley

1. Stir soup, tuna, water, carrots, onion and pepper into **CROCK-POT®** slow cooker. Place whole unpeeled egg on top. Cover; cook on LOW 4 to 5 hours or on HIGH 1½ to 3 hours.

2. Remove egg; stir in pasta. Cover; cook on HIGH ½ to 1 hour or until onion is tender. Meanwhile, mash egg in small bowl; mix in bread crumbs and parsley. Top casserole with bread crumb mixture.

Makes 6 servings

Note: This casserole calls for a raw egg. The egg will hard-cook in its shell in the **CROCK-POT®** slow cooker.

Quick and Easy Homemade Chicken and Dumplings

1 whole chicken (3 to
    5 pounds), cut into pieces
2 large potatoes, cubed
3 medium carrots, chopped
1 cup chopped celery
4 tablespoons Italian
    seasoning, divided
1 whole bay leaf
1½ cups milk, divided
3 cups all-purpose flour,
    divided
3 tablespoons butter
½ teaspoon baking soda
    Salt and black pepper

1. Coat inside of **CROCK-POT®** slow cooker with nonstick cooking spray. Combine chicken, potatoes, carrots, celery, 3 tablespoons Italian seasoning and bay leaf in **CROCK-POT®** slow cooker; add enough water to cover chicken. Cover; cook on HIGH 4 hours.

2. Remove chicken to cutting board; shred with two forks. Stir ½ cup milk into 1 cup flour in small bowl until smooth. Whisk flour mixture into **CROCK-POT®** slow cooker; add shredded chicken.

3. Combine remaining 2 cups flour, butter, remaining 1 tablespoon Italian seasoning, baking soda, salt and pepper in medium bowl. Stir in remaining 1 cup milk to form soft dough. Drop dough by tablespoonfuls onto top of chicken mixture in **CROCK-POT®** slow cooker. Turn **CROCK-POT®** slow cooker to LOW. Cover; cook on LOW 30 minutes or until dumplings are cooked through. Remove and discard bay leaf.

Makes 10 to 12 servings

Super Meatball Sliders

(pictured on page 133)

1 can (15 ounces) whole berry cranberry sauce

1 can (about 15 ounces) tomato sauce

⅛ teaspoon red pepper flakes (optional)

2 pounds ground beef or turkey

¾ cup dry seasoned bread crumbs

1 egg, lightly beaten

1 package (1 ounce) dry onion soup mix

Nonstick cooking spray

Baby arugula leaves (optional)

24 small potato rolls or dinner rolls, split

6 slices (1 ounce *each*) provolone cheese, cut into quarters

1. Combine cranberry sauce, tomato sauce and red pepper flakes, if desired, in **CROCK-POT®** slow cooker. Cover; cook on LOW 3 to 4 hours.

2. Halfway through cooking time, prepare meatballs. Combine beef, bread crumbs, egg and soup mix in large bowl; mix well. Shape mixture into 24 meatballs (about 1¾ inches diameter). Spray medium skillet with cooking spray; heat over medium heat. Add meatballs; cook 8 to 10 minutes or until well browned on all sides. Remove meatballs to **CROCK-POT®** slow cooker.

3. Cover; cook on LOW 1 to 2 hours or until meatballs are no longer pink in centers. Place arugula leaves on bottom of rolls, if desired; top with meatballs and cheese. Spoon sauce over meatballs; cover with tops of rolls.

Makes 24 sliders

Cinnamon Roll and Sweet 'Tater Gratin

(pictured on page 132)

3 pounds sweet potatoes, cut into ¼-inch thick rounds

¾ cup (3 ounces) shredded mozzarella cheese

1 cup whipping cream

¼ to ½ teaspoon ground red pepper

Salt and black pepper

4 tablespoons (½ stick) butter, divided

1 can (about 12 ounces) refrigerated cinnamon roll dough

1. Coat inside of **CROCK-POT®** slow cooker with nonstick cooking spray. Arrange one third of sweet potatoes in **CROCK-POT®** slow cooker, overlapping slightly. Top with ¼ cup cheese. Repeat layers two additional times using sweet potatoes and cheese.

2. Combine cream, ground red pepper, salt and black pepper in small bowl; mix well. Pour cream mixture over sweet potato layers in **CROCK-POT®** slow cooker. Dot with 2 tablespoons butter.

3. Remove cinnamon roll dough from can; unroll into long strips. Set aside icing. Arrange strips of dough in lattice design on top of sweet potato layers, making sure edges are sealed. Dot dough with remaining 2 tablespoons butter. Cover; cook on HIGH 4 hours.

4. Turn off heat. Drizzle gratin with reserved icing. Let stand, uncovered, 15 minutes before serving.

Makes 10 servings

Vegetable-Stuffed Pork Chops

4 bone-in pork chops
  Salt and black pepper
1 can (about 15 ounces) corn,
  drained
1 green bell pepper, chopped
1 cup seasoned dry bread
  crumbs
1 small onion, chopped
½ cup uncooked converted
  long grain rice
1 can (8 ounces) tomato sauce

1. Cut pocket into each pork chop, cutting from edge to bone. Lightly season pockets with salt and black pepper. Combine corn, bell pepper, bread crumbs, onion and rice in large bowl. Stuff pork chops with rice mixture. Secure open side with toothpicks.

2. Place any remaining rice mixture in **CROCK-POT**® slow cooker; top with stuffed pork chops. Pour tomato sauce over pork chops. Cover; cook on LOW 8 to 10 hours.

3. Remove pork chops to serving platter. Remove and discard toothpicks. Serve with extra rice mixture.

Makes 4 servings

tip

Your butcher can cut a pocket in the pork chops to save you time and to ensure even cooking.

Ravioli Casserole

8 ounces pork or turkey
Italian sausage, casings
removed

½ cup minced onion

1½ cups marinara sauce

1 can (about 14 ounces)
Italian-style diced
tomatoes

2 packages (9 ounces *each*)
refrigerated meatless
ravioli, such as wild
mushroom or three
cheese, divided

1½ cups (6 ounces) shredded
mozzarella cheese,
divided

Chopped fresh Italian
parsley (optional)

1. Heat large skillet over medium-high heat. Brown sausage and onion 6 to 8 minutes, stirring to break up meat. Drain fat. Stir in marinara sauce and tomatoes; mix well. Remove from heat.

2. Coat inside of **CROCK-POT**® slow cooker with nonstick cooking spray. Spoon 1 cup sauce into **CROCK-POT**® slow cooker. Layer half of 1 package of ravioli over sauce; top with additional ½ cup sauce. Repeat layering once; top with ½ cup cheese. Repeat layering with remaining package ravioli and all remaining sauce, reserve remaining ½ cup cheese. Cover; cook on LOW 2½ to 3 hours or on HIGH 1½ to 2 hours or until sauce is heated through and ravioli is tender.

3. Sprinkle remaining ½ cup cheese over top of casserole. Cover; cook on HIGH 15 minutes or until cheese is melted. Garnish with parsley.

Makes 4 to 6 servings

Red Beans and Rice

2 cans (about 15 ounces *each*) red beans, undrained

1 can (about 14 ounces) diced tomatoes

½ cup chopped celery

½ cup chopped green bell pepper

½ cup chopped green onions

2 cloves garlic, minced

1 to 2 teaspoons hot pepper sauce

1 teaspoon Worcestershire sauce

1 whole bay leaf

3 cups hot cooked rice

1. Combine beans, tomatoes, celery, bell pepper, green onions, garlic, hot pepper sauce, Worcestershire sauce and bay leaf in **CROCK-POT®** slow cooker; stir to blend. Cover; cook on LOW 4 to 6 hours or on HIGH 2 to 3 hours.

2. Mash bean mixture slightly in **CROCK-POT®** slow cooker until mixture thickens. Cover; cook on HIGH ½ to 1 hour. Remove and discard bay leaf. Serve bean mixture over rice.

Makes 6 servings

Simple Barbecue Chicken

1 bottle (20 ounces) ketchup

⅔ cup packed brown sugar

⅔ cup cider vinegar

2 tablespoons chili powder

2 tablespoons tomato paste

1 tablespoon onion powder

2 teaspoons garlic powder

2 teaspoons liquid smoke (optional)

1 teaspoon hot pepper sauce (optional)

8 boneless, skinless chicken breasts (6 ounces *each*)

8 whole wheat rolls

1. Combine ketchup, brown sugar, vinegar, chili powder, tomato paste, onion powder, garlic powder, liquid smoke and hot pepper sauce, if desired, in **CROCK-POT®** slow cooker.

2. Add chicken. Cover; cook on LOW 4 to 6 hours or on HIGH 2 to 3 hours or until chicken is cooked through. Serve with rolls.

Makes 8 servings

Pulled Chicken Sandwiches: Shred the chicken and serve on whole wheat rolls or hamburger buns. Top with mixed greens or coleslaw.

Slow Cooker Pizza Casserole

1½ pounds ground beef

1 pound bulk pork sausage

4 jars (14 ounces *each*) pizza sauce

2 cups (8 ounces) shredded mozzarella cheese

2 cups grated Parmesan cheese

2 cans (4 ounces *each*) mushroom stems and pieces, drained

2 packages (3 ounces *each*) sliced pepperoni

½ cup finely chopped onion

½ cup finely chopped green bell pepper

1 clove garlic, minced

1 pound corkscrew pasta, cooked and drained

1. Brown beef and sausage in large nonstick skillet over medium-high heat 6 to 8 minutes, stirring to break up meat. Drain fat. Remove beef mixture to **CROCK-POT**® slow cooker.

2. Add pizza sauce, cheeses, mushrooms, pepperoni, onion, bell pepper and garlic; stir to blend. Cover; cook on LOW 3½ hours or on HIGH 2 hours.

3. Stir in pasta. Cover; cook on HIGH 15 to 20 minutes or until pasta is heated through.

Makes 6 servings

Ham and Potato Casserole

1½ pounds red potatoes,
    unpeeled and sliced

8 ounces thinly sliced deli ham

2 poblano chile peppers, cut
    into thin slices

2 tablespoons olive oil

1 tablespoon dried oregano

¼ teaspoon salt

1 cup (4 ounces) shredded
    Monterey Jack cheese

2 tablespoons finely chopped
    fresh cilantro

1. Combine potatoes, ham, chile peppers, oil, oregano and salt in **CROCK-POT**® slow cooker; stir to blend. Cover; cook on LOW 7 hours or on HIGH 4 hours.

2. Remove potato mixture to large serving platter. Sprinkle with cheese and cilantro; let stand 3 minutes or until cheese is melted.

Makes 6 servings

Easy Family Burritos

(pictured on page 132)

1 boneless beef chuck
    shoulder roast
    (2 to 3 pounds)*

1 jar (24 ounces) *or* 2 jars
    (16 ounces *each*) salsa

Flour tortillas, warmed

**Optional toppings: shredded
    lettuce, diced tomato
    and/or diced onion**

1. Place beef in **CROCK-POT**® slow cooker; top with salsa. Cover; cook on LOW 8 to 10 hours.

2. Remove beef to cutting board; shred with two forks. Return to cooking liquid; mix well. Cover; cook on LOW 1 to 2 hours or until heated through. Serve in tortillas. Top as desired.

Makes 8 servings

*Unless you have a 5-, 6- or 7-quart CROCK-POT® slow cooker, cut any roast larger than 2½ pounds in half so it cooks completely.

Ham and Potato Casserole

Boneless Chicken Cacciatore

Olive oil

6 boneless, skinless chicken breasts, sliced in half horizontally

4 cups tomato-basil pasta sauce

1 cup coarsely chopped yellow onion

1 cup coarsely chopped green bell pepper

1 can (6 ounces) sliced mushrooms

¼ cup chicken broth

2 teaspoons minced garlic

2 teaspoons dried oregano

2 teaspoons dried thyme

2 teaspoons salt

2 teaspoons black pepper

Hot cooked pasta

1. Heat oil in large skillet over medium heat. Add chicken; cook 6 to 8 minutes or until browned on both sides. Remove to **CROCK-POT**® slow cooker using slotted spoon.

2. Add pasta sauce, onion, bell pepper, mushrooms, broth, garlic, oregano, thyme, salt and black pepper to **CROCK-POT**® slow cooker; stir well to blend. Cover; cook on LOW 5 to 7 hours or on HIGH 2 to 3 hours. Serve over pasta.

Makes 6 servings

Mini Puttanesca Meatballs and Spaghetti

1 pound ground turkey
  or lean ground beef

¼ cup seasoned dry bread
  crumbs

1 egg

1 jar (24 to 26 ounces)
  marinara sauce

½ cup coarsely chopped pitted
  kalamata olives

2 tablespoons drained capers

½ to ¾ teaspoon red pepper
  flakes

6 ounces hot cooked spaghetti

¼ cup chopped fresh basil or
  Italian parsley

1. Preheat oven to 425°F. Combine turkey, bread crumbs and egg in large bowl; mix well. Shape into 24 (1-inch) meatballs; place on foil-lined baking sheet. Bake 15 to 18 minutes or until browned and no longer pink in center.

2. Coat inside of 2-quart **CROCK-POT**® slow cooker with nonstick cooking spray. Combine marinara sauce, olives, capers and red pepper flakes in **CROCK-POT**® slow cooker. Stir in meatballs. Cover; cook on LOW 3 to 4 hours or on HIGH 1½ to 2 hours. Serve sauce and meatballs with spaghetti. Top with basil.

Makes 8 servings

Chicken Cordon Blue Dinner

4 boneless, skinless chicken breasts (1 pound), pounded thin

½ teaspoon salt

½ teaspoon black pepper

1 tablespoon extra virgin olive oil

2 cups water

1 can (10¾ ounces) cream of mushroom soup

1 cup uncooked rice

¼ cup Dijon mustard

2 cups chopped ham

1 cup (4 ounces) shredded Swiss cheese

1 green onion, chopped

1. Season chicken with salt and pepper. Heat oil in large skillet over medium-high heat. Add chicken; cook 3 minutes on each side or until browned.

2. Place water, soup and rice in **CROCK-POT®** slow cooker; top with chicken. Cover; cook on LOW 4 hours.

3. Remove lid and brush chicken with mustard; top with ham and cheese. Cover; cook on LOW 30 minutes or until heated through. Garnish with green onion.

Makes 4 servings

Sloppy Joe Sliders

12 ounces ground beef

1 can (about 14 ounces) stewed tomatoes with Mexican seasonings

½ cup frozen mixed vegetables, thawed

½ cup chopped green bell pepper

3 tablespoons ketchup

2 teaspoons Worcestershire sauce

1 teaspoon ground cumin

1 teaspoon cider vinegar

24 mini whole wheat rolls, split and warmed

1. Brown beef in large skillet over medium-high heat 6 to 8 minutes, stirring to break up meat. Remove to **CROCK-POT**® slow cooker using slotted spoon. Add tomatoes, mixed vegetables, pepper, ketchup, Worcestershire sauce, cumin and vinegar.

2. Cover; cook on LOW 2 to 3 hours or until vegetables are tender. Spoon evenly onto each roll.

Makes 24 mini sandwiches

Cheesy Broccoli Casserole

2 packages (10 ounces *each*) frozen chopped broccoli, thawed

1 can (10½ ounces) condensed cream of celery soup, undiluted

1¼ cups (5 ounces) shredded sharp Cheddar cheese, divided

¼ cup minced onion

1 teaspoon paprika

1 teaspoon hot pepper sauce

½ teaspoon celery seeds

1 cup crushed potato chips or saltine crackers

1. Coat inside of **CROCK-POT®** slow cooker with nonstick cooking spray. Combine broccoli, soup, 1 cup cheese, onion, paprika, hot pepper sauce and celery seeds in **CROCK-POT®** slow cooker; mix well. Cover; cook on LOW 5 to 6 hours or on HIGH 2½ to 3 hours.

2. Uncover; sprinkle top with potato chips and remaining ¼ cup cheese. Cook, uncovered, on LOW 30 to 60 minutes or on HIGH 15 to 30 minutes or until cheese is melted.

Makes 4 to 6 servings

Variations: Substitute thawed chopped spinach for the broccoli and top with crushed crackers or spicy croutons.

Chunky Ranch Potatoes (page 194)

French Carrot Medley (page 176)

Satisfying Sides

Corn on the Cob with Garlic Herb Butter (page 176)

Sunshine Squash

1 butternut squash (about 2 pounds), seeded and diced

1 can (about 15 ounces) corn, drained

1 can (about 14 ounces) diced tomatoes

1 onion, coarsely chopped

1 green bell pepper, cut into 1-inch pieces

½ cup chicken broth

1 mild green chile, coarsely chopped

1 clove garlic, minced

½ teaspoon salt

¼ teaspoon black pepper

1 tablespoon plus 1½ teaspoons tomato paste

1. Combine squash, corn, diced tomatoes, onion, bell pepper, broth, green chile, garlic, salt and black pepper in **CROCK-POT**® slow cooker. Cover; cook on LOW 6 hours.

2. Remove about ¼ cup cooking liquid; blend liquid with tomato paste in small bowl. Stir mixture into **CROCK-POT**® slow cooker. Cover; cook on LOW 30 minutes or until mixture is slightly thickened and heated through.

Makes 6 to 8 servings

Cauliflower Mash

2 heads cauliflower
  (8 cups florets)
1 tablespoon butter
1 tablespoon half-and-half
  or whole milk
  Salt
  Sprigs fresh Italian parsley
  (optional)

1. Arrange cauliflower in **CROCK-POT**® slow cooker; add enough water to fill **CROCK-POT**® slow cooker about 2 inches. Cover; cook on LOW 5 to 6 hours. Drain well.

2. Place cooked cauliflower in food processor or blender; process until almost smooth. Add butter; process until smooth. Add half-and-half as needed to reach desired consistency. Season with salt. Garnish with parsley.

Makes 6 servings

tip

You may substitute the same amount of cream, buttermilk or chicken broth for the half-and-half.

Candied Sweet Potatoes

3 medium sweet potatoes (1½ to 2 pounds), sliced into ½-inch rounds

½ cup water

¼ cup (½ stick) butter, cut into pieces

¼ cup plus 2 tablespoons sugar

1 tablespoon vanilla

1 teaspoon nutmeg

Combine sweet potatoes, water, butter, sugar, vanilla and nutmeg in **CROCK-POT®** slow cooker; mix well. Cover; cook on LOW 7 hours or on HIGH 4 hours.

Makes 4 servings

Red Cabbage and Apples

1 small head red cabbage, cored and thinly sliced

1 large apple, peeled and grated

¾ cup sugar

½ cup red wine vinegar

1 teaspoon ground cloves

½ cup bacon, crisp-cooked and crumbled

Fresh apple slices (optional)

Combine cabbage, grated apples, sugar, vinegar and cloves in **CROCK-POT®** slow cooker. Cover; cook on HIGH 6 hours, stirring halfway through cooking time. Sprinkle with bacon. Garnish with apple slices.

Makes 6 servings

Candied Sweet Potatoes

Buttery Vegetable Gratin

3 leeks, halved lengthwise and cut into 1-inch pieces

1 red bell pepper, cut into ½-inch pieces

5 tablespoons unsalted butter, divided

4 tablespoons grated Parmesan cheese, divided

1 teaspoon fresh thyme, divided

¾ teaspoon salt, divided

¼ plus ⅛ teaspoon black pepper, divided

2 zucchini (about 1½ pounds total), cut into ¾-inch-thick slices

2 yellow squash (about 1½ pounds total), cut into ¾-inch-thick slices

1½ cups fresh bread crumbs

1. Coat inside of **CROCK-POT**® slow cooker with nonstick cooking spray. Place leeks and bell pepper in bottom of **CROCK-POT**® slow cooker. Dot with 1 tablespoon butter, 1 tablespoon cheese, ½ teaspoon thyme, ¼ teaspoon salt and ⅛ teaspoon black pepper.

2. Arrange zucchini in single layer over leeks, overlapping as necessary. Dot with 1 tablespoon butter, 1 tablespoon cheese, remaining ½ teaspoon thyme, ¼ teaspoon salt and ⅛ teaspoon black pepper.

3. Arrange yellow squash in single layer over zucchini, overlapping as necessary. Dot with 1 tablespoon butter, remaining 2 tablespoons cheese, ¼ teaspoon salt and ⅛ teaspoon black pepper. Cover; cook on LOW 4 to 5 hours or until vegetables are soft.

4. Meanwhile, melt remaining 2 tablespoons butter in large skillet over medium-high heat. Add bread crumbs; cook and stir 6 minutes or until crisp and golden brown. Remove to medium bowl; set aside to cool. Sprinkle over vegetable mixture just before serving.

Makes 12 servings

Corn on the Cob with Garlic Herb Butter

(pictured on page 167)

4 to 5 ears of corn, husked

½ cup (1 stick) unsalted butter, softened

3 to 4 cloves garlic, minced

2 tablespoons finely minced fresh Italian parsley

Salt and black pepper

1. Place each ear of corn on a piece of foil. Combine butter, garlic and parsley in small bowl; spread onto corn. Season with salt and pepper; tightly seal foil.

2. Place in **CROCK-POT**® slow cooker, overlapping ears, if necessary. Add enough water to come one fourth of the way up each ear. Cover; cook on LOW 4 to 5 hours or on HIGH 2 to 2½ hours.

Makes 4 to 5 servings

French Carrot Medley

(pictured on page 166)

2 cups sliced carrots

¾ cup unsweetened orange juice

1 can (4 ounces) sliced mushrooms, undrained

4 stalks celery, sliced

2 tablespoons chopped onion

½ teaspoon dried dill weed

Salt and black pepper

¼ cup cold water

2 teaspoons cornstarch

1. Combine carrots, orange juice, mushrooms, celery, onion, dill weed, salt and pepper in **CROCK-POT**® slow cooker. Cover; cook on LOW 3 to 4 hours or on HIGH 2 hours.

2. Stir water into cornstarch in small bowl until smooth. Whisk into cooking liquid in **CROCK-POT**® slow cooker. Cover; cook on HIGH 15 minutes or until sauce is thickened. Spoon sauce over vegetable mixture before serving.

Makes 6 servings

Chili Barbecue Beans

1 cup dried **Great Northern beans, rinsed and sorted**

1 cup dried **red beans or dried kidney beans, rinsed and sorted**

1 cup dried **baby lima beans, rinsed and sorted**

3 cups **water**

8 slices **bacon, crisp-cooked and crumbled** *or* 8 ounces **smoked sausage, sliced**

¼ cup packed **brown sugar**

2 tablespoons **minced onion**

2 cubes **beef bouillon**

1 teaspoon **dry mustard**

1 teaspoon **chili powder**

1 teaspoon **minced garlic**

½ teaspoon **black pepper**

¼ teaspoon **red pepper flakes**

2 whole **bay leaves**

1 to 1½ cups **barbecue sauce**

1. Place beans in large bowl and add enough cold water to cover by at least 2 inches. Soak 6 to 8 hours or overnight.* Drain beans; discard water.

2. Combine soaked beans, 3 cups water, bacon, brown sugar, onion, bouillon cubes, mustard, chili powder, garlic, black pepper, red pepper flakes and bay leaves in **CROCK-POT**® slow cooker. Cover; cook on LOW 8 to 10 hours.

3. Stir in barbecue sauce. Cover; cook on LOW 1 hour or until heated through. Remove and discard bay leaves. Serve warm.

*To quick soak beans, place beans in large saucepan and cover with water. Bring to a boil over high heat. Boil 2 minutes. Remove from heat; let soak, covered, 1 hour.

Makes 8 to 10 servings

Cran-Orange Acorn Squash

5 tablespoons instant brown rice

3 tablespoons minced onion

3 tablespoons diced celery

3 tablespoons dried cranberries

Pinch ground sage

3 small acorn or carnival squash, cut in half

1 teaspoon butter, cut into cubes

3 tablespoons orange juice

½ cup warm water

1. Combine rice, onion, celery, cranberries and sage in small bowl. Stuff each squash with rice mixture; dot with butter. Pour ½ tablespoon orange juice into each squash half over stuffing.

2. Stand squash in **CROCK-POT®** slow cooker. Pour water into **CROCK-POT®** slow cooker. Cover; cook on LOW 2½ hours or until squash is tender.

Makes 6 servings

Green Bean Casserole

2 packages (10 ounces *each*)
    frozen green beans,
    thawed
1 can (10½ ounces) condensed
    cream of mushroom
    soup, undiluted
1 tablespoon chopped fresh
    Italian parsley
1 tablespoon chopped roasted
    red peppers
1 teaspoon dried sage
½ teaspoon salt
½ teaspoon black pepper
¼ teaspoon ground nutmeg
½ cup toasted slivered
    almonds*

*To toast almonds, spread in single
layer in heavy skillet. Cook over
medium heat 1 to 2 minutes or until
nuts are lightly browned, stirring
frequently.

Combine green beans, soup, parsley, red peppers, sage, salt, black pepper and nutmeg in **CROCK-POT**® slow cooker. Cover; cook on LOW 3 to 4 hours. Sprinkle with almonds just before serving.

Makes 4 to 6 servings

Parmesan Potato Wedges

2 pounds red potatoes, unpeeled and cut into ½-inch wedges

¼ cup finely chopped yellow onion

1½ teaspoons dried oregano

½ teaspoon salt

¼ teaspoon black pepper

2 tablespoons butter, cubed

¼ cup grated Parmesan cheese

1. Layer potatoes, onion, oregano, salt and pepper in **CROCK-POT®** slow cooker; dot with butter. Cover; cook on HIGH 4 hours.

2. Remove potatoes to serving platter; sprinkle with cheese.

Makes 6 servings

tip

Freshly grated Parmesan cheese will have a much better flavor and texture than the canned versions.

Orange-Spice Glazed Carrots

1 package (32 ounces) baby
    carrots
½ cup packed light brown
    sugar
½ cup orange juice
3 tablespoons butter
¾ teaspoon ground cinnamon
¼ teaspoon ground nutmeg
¼ cup cold water
2 tablespoons cornstarch

1. Combine carrots, brown sugar, orange juice, butter, cinnamon and nutmeg in **CROCK-POT**® slow cooker. Cover; cook on LOW 3½ to 4 hours or until carrots are crisp-tender.

2. Spoon carrots into large serving bowl. Turn **CROCK-POT**® slow cooker to HIGH.

3. Stir water into cornstarch in small bowl until smooth. Whisk into **CROCK-POT**® slow cooker. Cover; cook on HIGH 15 minutes or until thickened. Spoon over carrots.

Makes 6 servings

Collard Greens

1 tablespoon olive oil
3 turkey necks
5 bunch collard greens,
    stemmed and chopped
5 cups chicken broth
1 small onion, chopped
2 cloves garlic, minced
1 tablespoon apple cider
    vinegar
1 teaspoon sugar
    Salt and black pepper
    Red pepper flakes (optional)

1. Heat oil in large skillet over medium-high heat. Add turkey necks; cook and stir 3 to 5 minutes or until brown.

2. Combine turkey necks, collard greens, broth, onion and garlic in **CROCK-POT**® slow cooker. Cover; cook on LOW 5 to 6 hours. Remove and discard turkey necks. Stir in vinegar, sugar, salt, black pepper and red pepper flakes, if desired.

Makes 12 servings

Orange-Spice Glazed Carrots

Rustic Cheddar Mashed Potatoes

2 pounds russet potatoes, diced

1 cup water

⅓ cup butter, cubed

½ to ¾ cup milk

1¼ teaspoons salt

½ teaspoon black pepper

¾ cup (3 ounces) shredded Cheddar cheese

½ cup finely chopped green onions

1. Combine potatoes and water in **CROCK-POT®** slow cooker; dot with butter. Cover; cook on LOW 6 hours or on HIGH 3 hours.

2. Remove potatoes to large bowl. Beat potatoes with electric mixer at medium speed 5 minutes or until creamy. Add milk, salt and pepper; beat until smooth.

3. Stir in cheese and green onions. Turn off heat. Cover; let stand 15 minutes.

Makes 8 servings

Skinny Corn Bread

1¼ cups all-purpose flour

¾ cup yellow cornmeal

¼ cup sugar

1 teaspoon baking powder

1 teaspoon baking soda

¼ teaspoon seasoned salt

1 cup buttermilk

1 egg

¼ cup canola oil

1. Coat inside of 3-quart **CROCK-POT®** slow cooker with nonstick cooking spray.

2. Combine flour, cornmeal, sugar, baking powder, baking soda and seasoned salt in large bowl. Make well in center of dry mixture. Pour buttermilk, egg and oil in well; stir just until moistened. Pour mixture into **CROCK-POT®** slow cooker.

3. Cover; cook on LOW 3 to 4 hours or on HIGH 45 minutes to 1½ hours or until edge is golden and knife inserted into center comes out clean. Remove stoneware from **CROCK-POT®** slow cooker. Cool on wire rack 10 minutes. Remove bread from stoneware; cool completely.

Makes 8 servings

Rustic Cheddar Mashed Potatoes

Slow-Cooked Succotash

2 teaspoons canola oil
1 cup diced onion
1 cup diced green bell pepper
1 cup diced celery
1 teaspoon paprika
1½ cups frozen corn, thawed
1½ cups frozen lima beans, thawed
1 cup canned diced tomatoes
2 teaspoons dried parsley flakes *or* 1 tablespoon minced fresh Italian parsley
½ teaspoon salt
½ teaspoon black pepper

1. Heat oil in large skillet over medium heat. Add onion, bell pepper and celery; cook and stir 5 minutes or until onion is translucent and bell pepper and celery are crisp-tender. Stir in paprika.

2. Combine onion mixture, corn, beans, tomatoes, parsley, salt and black pepper in **CROCK-POT®** slow cooker; stir to blend. Cover; cook on LOW 6 to 8 hours or on HIGH 3 to 4 hours.

Makes 8 servings

Escalloped Corn

2 tablespoons butter

½ cup chopped onion

3 tablespoons all-purpose flour

1 cup milk

4 cups frozen corn, thawed and divided

½ teaspoon salt

½ teaspoon dried thyme

¼ teaspoon black pepper

⅛ teaspoon ground nutmeg

Sprigs fresh thyme (optional)

1. Melt butter in medium saucepan over medium heat. Add onion; cook and stir 5 minutes or until tender. Add flour; cook and stir 1 minute. Stir in milk. Bring to a boil; cook and stir 1 minute or until thickened.

2. Process 2 cups corn in food processor or blender until coarsely chopped. Combine milk mixture, chopped and remaining whole corn, salt, dried thyme, pepper and nutmeg in **CROCK-POT®** slow cooker; stir to blend. Cover; cook on LOW 3½ to 4 hours or until mixture is bubbly around edge. Garnish with fresh thyme.

Makes 6 servings

tip

Always taste your dish before serving and adjust the seasonings, including salt and pepper.

Cheesy Cauliflower

3 pounds cauliflower florets

¼ cup water

5 tablespoons unsalted butter

1 cup finely chopped onion

6 tablespoons all-purpose flour

¼ teaspoon dry mustard

2 cups milk

2 cups (8 ounces) shredded sharp Cheddar cheese

Salt and black pepper

1. Coat inside of **CROCK-POT®** slow cooker with nonstick cooking spray. Add cauliflower and water.

2. Melt butter in medium saucepan over medium-high heat. Add onion; cook 4 to 5 minutes or until slightly softened. Add flour and mustard; cook and stir 3 minutes or until well combined. Whisk in milk until smooth. Bring to a boil; cook 1 to 2 minutes or until thickened. Stir in cheese, salt and pepper. Cook and stir until cheese is melted.

3. Pour cheese mixture into **CROCK-POT®** slow cooker. Cover; cook on LOW 4 to 4½ hours.

Makes 8 to 10 servings

Coconut-Lime Sweet Potatoes

2½ pounds sweet potatoes, cut into 1-inch pieces

8 ounces shredded carrots

¾ cup shredded coconut, divided

1 tablespoon unsalted butter, melted

3 tablespoons sugar

½ teaspoon salt

⅓ cup walnuts, toasted, coarsely chopped and divided*

2 teaspoons grated lime peel

To toast walnuts, spread in single layer in small skillet. Cook and stir over medium heat 1 to 2 minutes or until lightly browned.

1. Combine sweet potatoes, carrots, ½ cup coconut, butter, sugar and salt in **CROCK-POT®** slow cooker. Cover; cook on LOW 5 to 6 hours. Remove to large bowl.

2. Mash sweet potatoes with potato masher. Stir in 3 tablespoons walnuts and lime peel. Sprinkle with remaining walnuts and ¼ cup coconut.

Makes 8 servings

Cheesy Cauliflower

Slow-Good Apples and Carrots

6 carrots, sliced into ½-inch
slices

4 apples, peeled, cored and
sliced

¼ cup plus 1 tablespoon
all-purpose flour

1 tablespoon packed brown
sugar

½ teaspoon ground nutmeg

1 tablespoon butter, cubed

½ cup orange juice

Layer carrots and apples in **CROCK-POT®** slow cooker. Combine flour, brown sugar and nutmeg in small bowl; sprinkle over carrots and apples. Dot with butter; pour in juice. Cover; cook on LOW 3½ to 4 hours or until carrots are crisp-tender.

Makes 6 servings

Chunky Ranch Potatoes

(pictured on page 166)

3 pounds unpeeled red
potatoes, quartered

1 cup water

½ cup prepared ranch dressing

½ cup grated Parmesan or
Cheddar cheese

¼ cup minced fresh chives

1. Place potatoes in **CROCK-POT®** slow cooker. Add water. Cover; cook on LOW 7 to 9 hours or on HIGH 4 to 6 hours.

2. Stir in ranch dressing, cheese and chives. Break up potatoes into large pieces.

Makes 8 servings

Slow-Good Apples and Carrots

CROCK·POT

· THE ORIGINAL SLOW COOKER ·

Chicken Azteca (page 230)

Poblano Creamed Corn (page 216)

Mexican Fiesta

Shredded Beef Wraps (page 220)

Pollo Ranchero (Country Chicken)

1 whole chicken (2 to 3 pounds),
cut into pieces

5 cups chopped tomatoes

2 cups water

1 cup chopped ham

1 large onion, chopped

2 jalapeño peppers, minced*

4 sprigs fresh tarragon

2 tablespoons seasoned salt

2 tablespoons onion powder

2 tablespoons garlic powder

2 tablespoons tomato paste

Hot cooked rice

*Jalapeño peppers can sting and
irritate the skin, so wear rubber gloves
when handling peppers and do not
touch your eyes.

Combine chicken, tomatoes, water, ham, onion,
jalapeño peppers, tarragon, seasoned salt, onion
powder, garlic powder and tomato paste in
CROCK-POT® slow cooker. Cover; cook on
HIGH 3 to 4 hours. Serve over rice.

Makes 4 servings

tip

It is never recommended to
preheat the **CROCK-POT®** slow
cooker base before adding the
inner stoneware.

Arroz con Queso

1 can (16 ounces) crushed tomatoes, undrained

1 can (about 15 ounces) black beans, rinsed and drained

1½ cups uncooked converted long grain rice

1 onion, chopped

1 cup cottage cheese

1 can (4 ounces) chopped mild green chiles

2 tablespoons vegetable oil

3 teaspoons minced garlic

2 cups shredded Monterey Jack cheese, divided

Combine tomatoes, beans, rice, onion, cottage cheese, chiles, oil, garlic and 1 cup cheese in **CROCK-POT®** slow cooker; stir to blend. Cover; cook on LOW 6 to 9 hours or until liquid is absorbed. Sprinkle with remaining 1 cup cheese before serving.

Makes 8 to 10 servings

Chicken and Spicy Black Bean Tacos

1 can (about 15 ounces)
  black beans, rinsed and
  drained

1 can (10 ounces) diced
  tomatoes with mild green
  chiles, drained

1½ teaspoons chili powder

¾ teaspoon ground cumin

1 tablespoon plus 1 teaspoon
  extra virgin olive oil,
  divided

12 ounces boneless, skinless
  chicken breasts

12 crisp corn taco shells

Optional toppings: shredded
  lettuce, diced tomatoes,
  shredded Cheddar
  cheese, sour cream and/
  or sliced black olives

1. Coat inside of **CROCK-POT®** slow cooker with nonstick cooking spray. Add beans and tomatoes with chiles. Combine chili powder, cumin and 1 teaspoon oil in small bowl; rub onto chicken. Place chicken in **CROCK-POT®** slow cooker. Cover; cook on HIGH 1¾ hours.

2. Remove chicken to cutting board and slice. Remove bean mixture to large bowl using slotted spoon. Stir in remaining 1 tablespoon oil.

3. To serve, warm taco shells according to package directions. Fill with equal amounts of bean mixture and chicken. Top as desired.

Makes 4 servings

Mexican Corn Bread Pudding

1 can (about 14¾ ounces)
    cream-style corn

¾ cup yellow cornmeal

1 can (4 ounces) diced mild
    green chiles

2 eggs

2 tablespoons sugar

2 tablespoons vegetable oil

2 teaspoons baking powder

¾ teaspoon salt

½ cup (2 ounces) shredded
    Cheddar cheese

1. Coat inside of 2-quart **CROCK-POT®** slow cooker with nonstick cooking spray. Combine corn, cornmeal, chiles, eggs, sugar, oil, baking powder and salt in medium bowl; stir to blend. Pour into **CROCK-POT®** slow cooker.

2. Cover; cook on LOW 2 to 2½ hours or until center is set. Turn off heat. Sprinkle cheese over top. Cover; let stand 5 minutes or until cheese is melted.

Makes 8 servings

Mexican Chili Chicken

2 medium green bell peppers,
   cut into thin strips

1 large onion, quartered and
   thinly sliced

4 chicken thighs

4 chicken drumsticks

1 tablespoon chili powder

2 teaspoons dried oregano

1 jar (16 ounces) chipotle salsa

½ cup ketchup

2 teaspoons ground cumin

½ teaspoon salt

   Hot cooked egg noodles

1. Place bell peppers and onion in **CROCK-POT**® slow cooker; top with chicken. Sprinkle chili powder and oregano evenly over chicken. Add salsa. Cover; cook on LOW 7 to 8 hours or on HIGH 2 to 3 hours.

2. Remove chicken to large serving bowl; cover with foil to keep warm. Stir ketchup, cumin and salt into cooking liquid. Cook, uncovered, on HIGH 15 minutes or until heated through.

3. Pour mixture over chicken. Serve chicken and sauce over noodles.

Makes 4 servings

tip

For thicker sauce, stir
2 tablespoons water into
1 tablespoon cornstarch in
small bowl until smooth. Stir
into cooking liquid with
ketchup, cumin and salt.

Chili Verde

1 tablespoon vegetable oil

1 to 2 pounds boneless pork chops

2 cups sliced carrots

1 jar (24 ounces) mild green salsa

1 cup chopped onion

1. Heat oil in large skillet over medium-low heat. Add pork; cook 3 to 5 minutes or until browned on both sides.

2. Place carrot slices in bottom of **CROCK-POT®** slow cooker. Place pork on top of carrots. Pour salsa over pork. Add onion. Cover; cook on HIGH 6 to 8 hours.

Makes 4 to 8 servings

Serving Suggestion: You can also shred this delicious pork recipe and serve it in tortillas with assorted toppings.

Layered Mexican-Style Casserole

2 cans (about 15 ounces *each*) hominy, drained*

1 can (about 15 ounces) black beans, rinsed and drained

1 can (about 14 ounces) diced tomatoes with garlic, basil and oregano

1 cup thick and chunky salsa

1 can (6 ounces) tomato paste

½ teaspoon ground cumin

3 (9-inch) flour tortillas

2 cups (8 ounces) shredded Monterey Jack cheese

¼ cup sliced black olives

*Hominy is corn that has been treated to remove the germ and hull. It can be found with the canned vegetables or beans in most supermarkets.

1. Prepare foil handles (see Note). Coat inside of **CROCK-POT**® slow cooker with nonstick cooking spray. Combine hominy, beans, tomatoes, salsa, tomato paste and cumin in large bowl; stir to blend.

2. Press 1 tortilla in bottom of **CROCK-POT**® slow cooker. Top with one third of hominy mixture and one third of cheese. Repeat layers. Press remaining tortilla on top. Top with remaining hominy mixture. Set aside remaining cheese.

3. Cover; cook on LOW 6 to 8 hours or on HIGH 2 to 3 hours. Turn off heat. Sprinkle with remaining cheese and olives. Cover; let stand 5 minutes. Pull out tortilla stack with foil handles.

Makes 6 servings

Note: To make foil handles, tear off three 18×2-inch strips of heavy-duty foil or use regular foil folded to double thickness. Crisscross foil strips in spoke design and place in **CROCK-POT**® slow cooker to make lifting of tortilla stack easier.

Pulled Pork Enchiladas

1 can (about 14 ounces) chicken broth

1 medium onion, chopped

2 minced canned chipotle peppers in adobo sauce, plus 1 tablespoon adobo sauce

2 cloves garlic, minced

2 teaspoons ground cumin

1 teaspoon ground cinnamon

1 teaspoon salt

½ teaspoon black pepper

1 boneless pork shoulder roast (5¾ pounds), trimmed

1 can (19 ounces) enchilada sauce, divided

1 jar prepared salsa

1 cup (4 ounces) shredded Mexican cheese blend, divided

1 can (4 ounces) diced mild green chiles

12 (6-inch) tortillas

Sour cream (optional)

Fresh cilantro (optional)

1. Combine broth, onion, chipotle peppers, adobo sauce and garlic in **CROCK-POT®** slow cooker. Combine cumin, cinnamon, salt and black pepper in small bowl; rub onto top of pork. Place pork in **CROCK-POT®** slow cooker, seasoned side up. Cover; cook on LOW 12 to 14 hours or on HIGH 6 to 7 hours or until pork is fork-tender.

2. Remove pork to cutting board. Shred pork with two forks. Measure 3 cups; reserve remaining pork for another use.

3. Preheat oven to 375°F. Combine 3 cups pork, 1 cup enchilada sauce, salsa and ¾ cup cheese in large bowl. Spread ½ cup enchilada sauce and diced green chiles in 13×9-inch baking dish. Spread ¼ cup pork mixture on each tortilla. Roll up and place seam side down in baking dish. Spread remaining enchilada sauce over tortillas.

4. Bake 20 minutes. Top with remaining ¼ cup cheese; bake 5 minutes or until cheese is melted. Serve with sour cream and cilantro, if desired.

Makes 6 servings

Mexican Carnitas

2 pounds boneless pork
    shoulder roast

1 tablespoon garlic salt

1 tablespoon black pepper

1½ teaspoons adobo seasoning

1 medium onion, chopped

½ cup water

¼ cup chopped fresh cilantro

    Juice of 2 medium limes

3 cloves garlic, minced

1 jar (16 ounces) green salsa

    Flour tortillas, warmed

    Optional toppings:
        chopped green bell
        pepper, tomatoes and/or
        red onion

1. Coat inside of **CROCK-POT**® slow cooker with nonstick cooking spray. Season pork with garlic salt, black pepper and adobo seasoning.

2. Place pork, salsa, onion, water, cilantro, lime juice and garlic in **CROCK-POT**® slow cooker. Cover; cook on LOW 4 to 5 hours. Serve in tortillas with desired toppings.

Makes 4 servings

Poblano Creamed Corn

(pictured on page 196)

- 2 whole poblano peppers
- 2 tablespoons olive oil
- 2 packages (16 ounces *each*) frozen corn, thawed
- 6 slices American cheese
- 1 package (8 ounces) cream cheese
- ¼ cup (½ stick) butter
- 3 tablespoons chicken broth or water
- 2 tablespoons chopped jalapeño pepper (optional)*
- Salt and black pepper
- Red pepper flakes or ground red pepper (optional)

*Jalapeño peppers can sting and irritate the skin, so wear rubber gloves when handling peppers and do not touch your eyes.

1. Preheat oven to 350°F. Spray small baking sheet with nonstick cooking spray. Place poblano peppers on prepared baking sheet; brush with oil. Bake 20 minutes or until outer skins loosen. When cool enough to handle, remove outer skins and mince poblano peppers.

2. Combine corn, American cheese, poblano peppers, cream cheese, butter, broth, jalapeño pepper, if desired, salt and black pepper in **CROCK-POT®** slow cooker. Cover; cook on LOW 4 to 5 hours. Garnish with red pepper flakes.

Makes 20 servings

Note: Bake additional poblano peppers 15 minutes. Cut lengthwise in half to create edible serving dishes for the corn.

Chipotle Chicken Casserole

1 pound boneless, skinless chicken thighs, cut into cubes

1½ cups chicken broth

1 can (about 15 ounces) navy beans, rinsed and drained

1 can (about 15 ounces) black beans, rinsed and drained

1 can (about 14 ounces) crushed tomatoes, undrained

½ cup orange juice

1 medium onion, diced

1 canned chipotle pepper in adobo sauce, minced

1 teaspoon salt

1 teaspoon ground cumin

1 whole bay leaf

¼ cup chopped fresh cilantro (optional)

Combine chicken, broth, beans, tomatoes, orange juice, onion, chipotle pepper, salt, cumin and bay leaf in **CROCK-POT®** slow cooker. Cover; cook on LOW 7 to 8 hours or on HIGH 3½ to 4 hours. Remove and discard bay leaf. Garnish with cilantro.

Makes 6 servings

Beefy Tostada Pie

2 teaspoons olive oil

1½ cups chopped onion

2 pounds ground beef

1 teaspoon chili powder

1 teaspoon ground cumin

1 teaspoon salt

2 cloves garlic, minced

1 can (15 ounces) tomato sauce

1 cup sliced black olives

8 flour tortillas

4 cups (16 ounces) shredded Cheddar cheese

Sour cream, salsa and chopped green onion (optional)

1. Heat oil in large skillet over medium heat. Add onion; cook and stir until tender. Add beef, chili powder, cumin, salt and garlic; cook and stir 6 to 8 minutes or until beef is browned. Drain fat. Stir in tomato sauce; cook until heated through. Stir in olives.

2. Make foil handles using three 18×2-inch strips of heavy-duty foil or use regular foil folded to double thickness. Crisscross foil in spoke design; place across bottom and up side of stoneware. Lay 1 tortilla on foil strips. Spread with meat sauce and ½ cup cheese. Top with another tortilla, meat sauce and cheese. Repeat layers five times, ending with tortilla. Cover; cook on HIGH 1½ hours.

3. To serve, lift out of **CROCK-POT®** slow cooker using foil handles and remove to large serving platter. Discard foil. Cut into wedges. Serve with sour cream, salsa and green onion, if desired.

Makes 4 to 6 servings

Posole

3 pounds pork tenderloin, cubed
3 cans (about 14 ounces *each*) white hominy, rinsed and drained
1 cup chili sauce

Combine pork, hominy and chili sauce in **CROCK-POT**® slow cooker; stir to blend. Cover; cook on LOW 10 hours or on HIGH 5 hours.

Makes 8 servings

Shredded Beef Wraps

(pictured on page 197)

1 beef flank steak or beef skirt steak (1 to 1½ pounds)
1 cup beef broth
½ cup sun-dried tomatoes (not packed in oil), chopped
3 to 4 cloves garlic, minced
¼ teaspoon ground cumin
4 (8-inch) flour tortillas
  Shredded lettuce, diced tomatoes and shredded Monterey Jack cheese (optional)

1. Cut flank steak into quarters. Place flank steak, broth, sun-dried tomatoes, garlic and cumin in **CROCK-POT**® slow cooker. Cover; cook on LOW 7 to 8 hours or until steak shreds easily.

2. Remove steak to cutting board; shred with two forks or cut into thin strips. Place remaining juices from **CROCK-POT**® slow cooker in blender or food processor; blend until sauce is smooth.

3. Spoon steak onto tortillas with small amount of sauce. Garnish with lettuce, diced tomatoes and cheese.

Makes 4 servings

Posole

Black Bean and Mushroom Chilaquiles

2 tablespoons olive oil

1 medium onion, chopped

1 medium green bell pepper, chopped

1 jalapeño or serrano pepper, seeded and minced*

2 cans (about 15 ounces *each*) black beans, rinsed and drained

1 can (about 14 ounces) diced tomatoes

10 ounces white mushrooms, cut into quarters

1½ teaspoons ground cumin

1½ teaspoons dried oregano

1 cup (4 ounces) shredded sharp white Cheddar cheese, plus additional for garnish

6 cups baked tortilla chips

*Jalapeño and serrano peppers can sting and irritate the skin, so wear rubber gloves when handling peppers and do not touch your eyes.

1. Heat oil in medium skillet over medium heat. Add onion, bell pepper and jalapeño pepper; cook until onion softens, stirring occasionally. Remove to **CROCK-POT®** slow cooker. Add beans, tomatoes, mushrooms, cumin and oregano. Cover; cook on LOW 6 hours or on HIGH 3 hours.

2. Sprinkle 1 cup Cheddar cheese over beans and mushrooms. Cover; cook on HIGH 15 minutes or until cheese is melted. Stir to combine.

3. For each serving, coarsely crush 1 cup tortilla chips into individual serving bowls. Top with black bean mixture. Garnish with additional cheese.

Makes 6 servings

Mexican-Style Spinach

3 packages (10 ounces *each*)
    frozen chopped spinach

1 tablespoon canola oil

1 onion, chopped

1 clove garlic, minced

2 Anaheim peppers, roasted,
    peeled and minced*

3 fresh tomatillos, roasted,
    husks removed and
    chopped**

6 tablespoons sour cream
    (optional)

*To roast peppers, heat medium skillet over medium heat. Add peppers; cook and stir until blackened all over. Place peppers in brown paper bag 2 to 5 minutes. Remove peppers from bag; scrape off charred skin. Cut off top and pull out core. Slice lengthwise; scrape off veins and any remaining seeds with a knife.

**To roast tomatillos, heat medium skillet over medium heat. Add tomatillos; cook and stir until husks are brown and interior flesh is soft. Remove from skillet. Remove and discard husks when cool enough to handle.

1. Place spinach in **CROCK-POT®** slow cooker. Heat oil in large skillet over medium heat. Add onion and garlic; cook and stir 5 minutes or until onion is soft but not browned. Add Anaheim peppers and tomatillos; cook 3 to 4 minutes.

2. Remove mixture to **CROCK-POT®** slow cooker. Cover; cook on LOW 4 to 6 hours. Serve with sour cream, if desired.

Makes 6 servings

Sweet and Spicy Pork Picadillo

1 tablespoon olive oil

1 yellow onion, cut into ¼-inch pieces

2 cloves garlic, minced

1 pound boneless pork country-style ribs, trimmed and cut into 1-inch cubes

1 can (about 14 ounces) diced tomatoes

3 tablespoons cider vinegar

2 canned chipotle peppers in adobo sauce, chopped*

½ cup raisins, chopped

½ teaspoon cumin

½ teaspoon ground cinnamon

Salt and black pepper

Hot cooked rice (optional)

Black beans (optional)

*You may substitute dried chipotle peppers, soaked in warm water about 20 minutes to soften before chopping.

1. Heat oil in large skillet over medium-low heat. Add onion and garlic; cook and stir 4 minutes or until translucent. Add pork; cook 5 to 7 minutes or until browned. Remove to **CROCK-POT**® slow cooker.

2. Combine tomatoes, vinegar, chipotle peppers, raisins, cumin and cinnamon in medium bowl. Pour over pork in **CROCK-POT**® slow cooker. Cover; cook on LOW 5 hours or on HIGH 3 hours.

3. Remove pork to cutting board; shred using two forks. Stir shredded pork and any accumulated juices from cutting board into **CROCK-POT**® slow cooker; stir to blend. Season with salt and pepper. Serve with rice and black beans, if desired.

Makes 4 servings

Carne Rellenos

1 can (4 ounces) whole mild
green chiles, drained

4 ounces cream cheese,
softened

1 flank steak (about 2 pounds)

1½ cups salsa verde

Hot cooked rice (optional)

1. Slit green chiles open on one side with sharp knife; stuff with cream cheese.

2. Open steak flat on sheet of waxed paper. Score steak; turn over. Lay stuffed chiles across unscored side of steak. Roll up; tie with kitchen string.

3. Place steak in **CROCK-POT**® slow cooker; pour in salsa. Cover; cook on LOW 6 to 8 hours or on HIGH 3 to 4 hours or until cooked through. Remove steak to cutting board. Let stand 10 to 15 minutes before slicing. Serve over rice with sauce, if desired.

Makes 6 servings

Chicken Azteca

(pictured on page 196)

2 cups frozen corn, thawed

1 can (about 15 ounces) black beans, rinsed and drained

1 cup chunky salsa, divided

1 clove garlic, minced

½ teaspoon ground cumin

4 boneless, skinless chicken breasts (about 1 pound)

1 package (8 ounces) cream cheese, cubed

Hot cooked rice

Shredded Cheddar cheese

1. Combine corn, beans, ½ cup salsa, garlic and cumin in **CROCK-POT®** slow cooker. Arrange chicken over top of corn mixture; pour remaining ½ cup salsa over chicken. Cover; cook on LOW 4 to 6 hours or on HIGH 2 to 3 hours.

2. Remove chicken to cutting board; cut into 1-inch pieces. Return chicken to **CROCK-POT®** slow cooker. Add cream cheese. Cover; cook on HIGH 15 to 20 minutes or until cream cheese is melted and blends into sauce. Serve chicken and sauce over rice. Top with Cheddar cheese.

Makes 4 servings

Fall-Apart Pork Roast with Mole

⅔ cup whole almonds

⅔ cup raisins

3 tablespoons vegetable oil, divided

½ cup chopped onion

4 cloves garlic, chopped

2¾ pounds boneless pork shoulder roast, well trimmed*

1 can (about 14 ounces) diced fire-roasted tomatoes or diced tomatoes

1 cup cubed bread, any variety

½ cup chicken broth

2 ounces Mexican chocolate, chopped

2 tablespoons canned chipotle peppers in adobo sauce, chopped

1 teaspoon salt

Chopped fresh cilantro (optional)

*Unless you have a 5-, 6- or 7-quart CROCK-POT® slow cooker, cut any roast larger than 2½ pounds in half so it cooks completely.

1. Heat large skillet over medium-high heat. Add almonds; cook and stir 3 to 4 minutes or until fragrant. Add raisins; cook and stir 1 to 2 minutes or until raisins begin to plump. Place half of almond mixture in large bowl. Reserve remaining half for garnish.

2. Heat 1 tablespoon oil in same skillet. Add onion and garlic; cook and stir 2 minutes or until softened. Add to almond mixture; set aside.

3. Heat remaining 2 tablespoons oil in same skillet. Add pork; cook 5 to 7 minutes or until browned on all sides. Remove to **CROCK-POT®** slow cooker.

4. Add tomatoes, bread, broth, chocolate, chipotle peppers and salt to almond mixture. Add tomato mixture in batches to food processor or blender; purée until smooth. Pour purée mixture over pork in **CROCK-POT®** slow cooker. Cover; cook on LOW 7 to 8 hours or on HIGH 3 to 4 hours.

5. Remove pork from **CROCK-POT®** slow cooker to large serving platter. Whisk sauce until smooth before spooning over pork. Garnish with reserved almond mixture and chopped cilantro.

Makes 6 servings

CROCK·POT®

◆ THE ORIGINAL SLOW COOKER ◆

Cherry Delight (page 242)

Fruit and Nut Baked Apples (page 239)

Delicious Desserts

Fudge and Cream Pudding Cake (page 244)

Peach Cobbler

2 packages (16 ounces *each*) frozen peaches, thawed and drained

½ cup plus 1 tablespoon sugar, divided

2 teaspoons ground cinnamon, divided

½ teaspoon ground nutmeg

¾ cup all-purpose flour

6 tablespoons butter, cubed

Whipped cream (optional)

1. Combine peaches, ½ cup sugar, 1½ teaspoons cinnamon and nutmeg in **CROCK-POT®** slow cooker; stir to blend.

2. Combine flour, remaining 1 tablespoon sugar and remaining ½ teaspoon cinnamon in small bowl. Cut in butter with pastry blender or two knives until mixture resembles coarse crumbs. Sprinkle over peach mixture. Cover; cook on HIGH 2 hours. Serve with whipped cream, if desired.

Makes 4 to 6 servings

tip

To make cleanup easier when cooking sticky or sugary foods, spray the inside of the **CROCK-POT®** slow cooker with nonstick cooking spray before adding ingredients.

S'mores Fondue

4 ounces semisweet chocolate chips

½ jar (about 3 ounces) marshmallow creme

3 tablespoons half-and-half

½ teaspoon vanilla

½ cup mini marshmallows

Bananas, strawberries, chocolate-covered pretzels, graham crackers and/or sliced apples

1. Combine chocolate chips, marshmallow creme and half-and-half in medium saucepan. Cook over medium heat 2 minutes or until melted and smooth, stirring constantly. Remove from heat. Stir in vanilla.

2. Coat inside of **CROCK-POT® LITTLE DIPPER®** slow cooker with nonstick cooking spray. Fill with warm fondue. Sprinkle with marshmallows and serve with fruit, pretzels and graham crackers.

Makes 1½ cups

Bananas Foster

12 bananas, cut into quarters

1 cup flaked coconut

1 cup dark corn syrup

⅔ cup butter, melted

¼ cup lemon juice

2 teaspoons grated lemon peel

2 teaspoons rum

1 teaspoon ground cinnamon

½ teaspoon salt

12 slices pound cake

1 quart vanilla ice cream

1. Combine bananas and coconut in **CROCK-POT®** slow cooker. Stir corn syrup, butter, lemon juice, lemon peel, rum, cinnamon and salt in medium bowl; pour over bananas.

2. Cover; cook on LOW 1 to 2 hours. To serve, arrange bananas on pound cake. Top with ice cream and warm sauce.

Makes 12 servings

S'mores Fondue

Pumpkin Custard

1 cup solid-pack pumpkin

½ cup packed brown sugar

2 eggs, beaten

½ teaspoon ground ginger

½ teaspoon grated lemon peel

½ teaspoon ground cinnamon, plus additional for garnish

1 can (12 ounces) evaporated milk

1. Combine pumpkin, brown sugar, eggs, ginger, lemon peel and ½ teaspoon cinnamon in large bowl. Stir in evaporated milk. Divide mixture among six ramekins or custard cups. Cover each cup tightly with foil.

2. Place ramekins in **CROCK-POT**® slow cooker. Pour water into **CROCK-POT**® slow cooker to come about ½ inch from top of ramekins. Cover; cook on LOW 4 hours.

3. Use tongs or slotted spoon to remove ramekins from **CROCK-POT**® slow cooker. Sprinkle with additional ground cinnamon. Serve warm.

Makes 6 servings

Variation: To make Pumpkin Custard in a single dish, pour custard into 1½-quart soufflé dish instead of ramekins. Cover with foil and place in **CROCK-POT**® slow cooker. (Place soufflé dish on two or three 18×2-inch strips of foil in **CROCK-POT**® slow cooker to make removal easier, if desired.) Add water to come 1½ inches from top of soufflé dish. Cover and cook as directed.

Fruit and Nut Baked Apples

(pictured on page 232)

4 large baking apples, such
    as Rome Beauty or
    Jonathan

1 tablespoon lemon juice

⅓ cup chopped dried apricots

⅓ cup chopped walnuts or
    pecans

3 tablespoons packed brown
    sugar

½ teaspoon ground cinnamon

2 tablespoons unsalted butter,
    melted

½ cup water

    Caramel ice cream topping
    (optional)

1. Scoop out center of each apple, leaving 1½-inch-wide cavity about ½ inch from bottom. Peel top of apple down about 1 inch. Brush peeled edges evenly with lemon juice. Mix apricots, walnuts, brown sugar and cinnamon in small bowl. Add butter; mix well. Spoon mixture evenly into apple cavities.

2. Pour water in bottom of **CROCK-POT®** slow cooker. Place 2 apples in bottom of **CROCK-POT®** slow cooker. Arrange remaining 2 apples above but not directly on top of bottom apples. Cover; cook on LOW 3 to 4 hours or until apples are tender. Serve warm or at room temperature with caramel ice cream topping, if desired.

Makes 4 servings

Brownie Bottoms

½ cup packed brown sugar

½ cup water

2 tablespoons unsweetened cocoa powder

2½ cups packaged brownie mix

1 package (2¾ ounces) instant chocolate pudding mix

½ cup milk chocolate chips

2 eggs, beaten

3 tablespoons butter, melted

Whipped cream or ice cream (optional)

1. Coat inside of **CROCK-POT**® slow cooker with nonstick cooking spray. Combine brown sugar, water and cocoa in small saucepan; bring to a boil over medium-high heat.

2. Meanwhile, combine brownie mix, pudding mix, chocolate chips, eggs and butter in medium bowl; stir until well blended. Spread batter in **CROCK-POT**® slow cooker; pour boiling sugar mixture over batter.

3. Cover; cook on HIGH 1½ hours. Turn off heat. Let stand 30 minutes. Top with whipped cream, if desired.

Makes 6 servings

Note: Recipe can be doubled for a 5-, 6- or 7-quart **CROCK-POT**® slow cooker.

Pineapple Rice Pudding

1 can (20 ounces) crushed pineapple in juice, undrained

1 can (13½ ounces) unsweetened coconut milk

1 can (12 ounces) evaporated milk

¾ cup uncooked Arborio rice

2 eggs, lightly beaten

¼ cup granulated sugar

¼ cup packed brown sugar

½ teaspoon ground cinnamon

¼ teaspoon salt

¼ teaspoon ground nutmeg

Toasted coconut (optional)

Fresh pineapple wedges (optional)

1. Combine crushed pineapple with juice, coconut milk, evaporated milk, rice, eggs, granulated sugar, brown sugar, cinnamon, salt and nutmeg in **CROCK-POT®** slow cooker; stir to blend. Cover; cook on HIGH 3 to 4 hours or until thickened and rice is tender.

2. Stir to blend. Serve warm or chilled. Garnish with coconut and pineapple slices.

Makes 8 servings

Note: To toast coconut, spread in a single layer in small heavy-bottomed skillet. Cook and stir over medium heat 1 to 2 minutes or until lightly browned. Remove from skillet; cool completely.

Cherry Delight

(pictured on page 232)

1 can (21 ounces) cherry pie filling

1 package (about 18 ounces) yellow cake mix

½ cup (1 stick) butter, melted

⅓ cup chopped walnuts

1. Place pie filling in **CROCK-POT®** slow cooker. Combine cake mix and butter in medium bowl. Spread evenly over pie filling. Sprinkle with walnuts.

2. Cover; cook on LOW 3 to 4 hours or on HIGH 1½ to 2 hours.

Makes 8 to 10 servings

Pineapple Rice Pudding

Fudge and Cream Pudding Cake

(pictured on page 233)

2 tablespoons unsalted butter

1 cup all-purpose flour

½ cup packed light brown sugar

5 tablespoons unsweetened cocoa powder, divided

2 teaspoons baking powder

½ teaspoon ground cinnamon

⅛ teaspoon salt

1 cup light cream

1 tablespoon vegetable oil

1 teaspoon vanilla

1½ cups hot water

½ cup packed dark brown sugar

Whipped cream or ice cream (optional)

1. Coat inside of 4½-quart **CROCK-POT®** slow cooker with butter. Combine flour, light brown sugar, 3 tablespoons cocoa, baking powder, cinnamon and salt in medium bowl. Add cream, oil and vanilla; stir well to combine. Pour batter into **CROCK-POT®** slow cooker.

2. Combine hot water, dark brown sugar and remaining 2 tablespoons cocoa in medium bowl; stir well. Pour sauce over cake batter. Do not stir. Cover; cook on HIGH 2 hours.

3. Spoon pudding cake onto plates. Serve with whipped cream, if desired.

Makes 8 to 10 servings

Apple Crumble Pot

FILLING

- 4 Granny Smith apples (about 2 pounds), cored and cut into 8 wedges *each*
- ⅔ cup packed dark brown sugar
- ½ cup dried cranberries
- 2 tablespoons biscuit baking mix
- 2 tablespoons butter, cubed
- 1½ teaspoons ground cinnamon
- 1 teaspoon vanilla
- ¼ teaspoon ground allspice

TOPPING

- 1 cup biscuit baking mix
- ½ cup rolled oats
- ⅓ cup packed dark brown sugar
- 3 tablespoons cold butter, cubed
- ½ cup chopped pecans
- Whipped cream or ice cream (optional)

1. Coat inside of **CROCK-POT**® slow cooker with nonstick cooking spray. For filling, combine apples, ⅔ cup brown sugar, cranberries, 2 tablespoons baking mix, butter, cinnamon, vanilla and allspice in **CROCK-POT**® slow cooker; toss gently to coat.

2. For topping, combine 1 cup baking mix, oats and ⅓ cup brown sugar in large bowl. Cut in 3 tablespoons butter with pastry blender or two knives until mixture resembles coarse crumbs. Sprinkle evenly over filling in **CROCK-POT**® slow cooker. Top with pecans. Cover; cook on HIGH 2¼ hours.

3. Turn off heat. Let stand, uncovered, 15 to 30 minutes before serving. Top with whipped cream, if desired.

Makes 6 to 8 servings

Easy Peach Buckle

2 packages (16 ounces *each*) frozen peach slices, thawed *or* 5 cups fresh peach slices

¼ cup granulated sugar

1¾ cups all-purpose flour

½ cup packed brown sugar

2 teaspoons baking powder

1 teaspoon ground cinnamon

1 teaspoon baking soda

¼ teaspoon salt

1⅓ cups buttermilk

6 tablespoons canola oil

1 teaspoon vanilla

1. Coat inside of 4½-quart **CROCK-POT®** slow cooker with nonstick cooking spray.

2. Toss peaches with granulated sugar; set aside.

3. Combine flour, brown sugar, baking powder, cinnamon, baking soda and salt in large bowl. Combine buttermilk, oil and vanilla in small bowl; mix well. Stir buttermilk mixture into flour mixture just until blended.

4. Spread batter evenly in **CROCK-POT®** slow cooker. Arrange peaches on batter. Cover; cook on HIGH 2½ hours or until buckle springs back when touched. Serve warm.

Makes 12 servings

tip

After cakes and breads have finished cooking, allow them to cool 5 to 10 minutes before removing them from the stoneware or baking pan.

Apple-Pecan Bread Pudding

8 cups bread, cubed

3 cups Granny Smith apples, cubed

1 cup chopped pecans

8 eggs

1 can (12 ounces) evaporated milk

1 cup packed brown sugar

½ cup apple cider or apple juice

2 teaspoons ground cinnamon

1 teaspoon ground nutmeg

1 teaspoon vanilla extract

½ teaspoon salt

½ teaspoon ground allspice

Ice cream (optional)

Caramel ice cream topping (optional)

1. Coat inside of **CROCK-POT**® slow cooker with nonstick cooking spray. Place bread cubes, apples and pecans in **CROCK-POT**® slow cooker.

2. Combine eggs, evaporated milk, brown sugar, apple cider, cinnamon, nutmeg, vanilla, salt and allspice in large bowl; mix well. Pour egg mixture in **CROCK-POT**® slow cooker. Cover; cook on LOW 3 hours. Serve with ice cream and top with caramel sauce, if desired.

Makes 8 servings

Metric Conversion Chart

VOLUME MEASUREMENTS (dry)

1/8 teaspoon = 0.5 mL
1/4 teaspoon = 1 mL
1/2 teaspoon = 2 mL
3/4 teaspoon = 4 mL
1 teaspoon = 5 mL
1 tablespoon = 15 mL
2 tablespoons = 30 mL
1/4 cup = 60 mL
1/3 cup = 75 mL
1/2 cup = 125 mL
2/3 cup = 150 mL
3/4 cup = 175 mL
1 cup = 250 mL
2 cups = 1 pint = 500 mL
3 cups = 750 mL
4 cups = 1 quart = 1 L

VOLUME MEASUREMENTS (fluid)

1 fluid ounce (2 tablespoons) = 30 mL
4 fluid ounces (1/2 cup) = 125 mL
8 fluid ounces (1 cup) = 250 mL
12 fluid ounces (1 1/2 cups) = 375 mL
16 fluid ounces (2 cups) = 500 mL

WEIGHTS (mass)

1/2 ounce = 15 g
1 ounce = 30 g
3 ounces = 90 g
4 ounces = 120 g
8 ounces = 225 g
10 ounces = 285 g
12 ounces = 360 g
16 ounces = 1 pound = 450 g

DIMENSIONS

1/16 inch = 2 mm
1/8 inch = 3 mm
1/4 inch = 6 mm
1/2 inch = 1.5 cm
3/4 inch = 2 cm
1 inch = 2.5 cm

OVEN TEMPERATURES

250°F = 120°C
275°F = 140°C
300°F = 150°C
325°F = 160°C
350°F = 180°C
375°F = 190°C
400°F = 200°C
425°F = 220°C
450°F = 230°C

BAKING PAN SIZES

Utensil	Size in Inches/Quarts	Metric Volume	Size in Centimeters
Baking or Cake Pan (square or rectangular)	8×8×2	2 L	20×20×5
	9×9×2	2.5 L	23×23×5
	12×8×2	3 L	30×20×5
	13×9×2	3.5 L	33×23×5
Loaf Pan	8×4×3	1.5 L	20×10×7
	9×5×3	2 L	23×13×7
Round Layer Cake Pan	8×1½	1.2 L	20×4
	9×1½	1.5 L	23×4
Pie Plate	8×1¼	750 mL	20×3
	9×1¼	1 L	23×3
Baking Dish or Casserole	1 quart	1 L	—
	1½ quarts	1.5 L	—
	2 quarts	2 L	—